KAISER STEEL

OF FONTANA

· TOGETHER WE BUILD ·

RIC A. DIAS

FOREWORD BY NICHOLAS R. CATALDO,
PRESIDENT OF SAN BERNARDINO HISTORICAL AND PIONEER SOCIETY

THE
History
PRESS

Published by The History Press
Charleston, SC
www.historypress.com

Copyright © 2022 by Ric A. Dias
All rights reserved

All images are courtesy of Fontana Historical Society, unless otherwise noted.

First published 2022

Manufactured in the United States

ISBN 9781467151498

Library of Congress Control Number: 2022935427

CONTENTS

FOREWORD

After the Japanese attack on Pearl Harbor in 1941, the United States started bracing itself for the international conflict to be known in history as World War II. Our country was short on steel for the building of needed ships, and before long, the sensational announcement came to San Bernardino County that Fontana, a railroad convergence located a safe distance from possible coastal bombardment, would become an ideal site for a steel mill in the war effort. A loan from the Reconstruction Finance Corporation enabled Henry Kaiser to establish a steel plant in that small town. Operations began on December 30, 1942, when Kaiser lit Blast Furnace No. 1 at a ceremony that brought distinguished guests from Washington, D.C. Forged artillery shells for overseas battlefields were manufactured at the mill. At the shell factory's peak, employees produced an estimated 150,000 heavy artillery shells monthly.

The impact of Kaiser Steel on the San Bernardino Valley had both an immediate effect during the war and a long-lasting one for many years. This essentially rural, agricultural area was transformed in a very short time into an industrial economy that would have lasting effects. Not only was the economy altered but also, in the long run, so was the delivery of health services—with development of the Kaiser Permanente Healthcare Program along with its hospitals and clinics. Kaiser Steel eventually became the largest steel producer west of the Mississippi River and employed a major workforce in the San Bernardino Valley until shutting waiting to hear about funding or acceptance? The answer is: too often. Shelly's unwavering support and constant encouragement to finish allowed this book project, decades in the making, to finally reach completion, and for that I will be forever grateful.

CHAPTER 1

"WHAT WE'VE BEEN NEEDING IS MORE SMOKE"

THE ORIGINS OF KAISER STEEL

FONTANA BEFORE KAISER STEEL

When it comes to the story of the area around what became Fontana, control of water has been key to success and growth. Therefore, it's no surprise that residents and boosters in the San Bernardino Valley in the nineteenth century developed water distribution companies. These interests formed the Semi-Tropic Land and Water Company in 1887 to centralize control over water and distribute land, capitalized with $3 million. Semi-Tropic purchased twenty-eight thousand acres of land (and accompanying water rights from Lytle Creek) and laid out several town sites, one of them being Fontana; *fontana* means "fountain" or "water source" in Italian. The company built the six-mile-long concrete Rialto Canal to bring the water efficiently from Lytle Creek to their development. Semi-Tropic subdivided the land primarily into twenty-acre plots and encouraged its new residents to grow fruit trees, particularly citrus, which thrived in the hot, sunny weather. But Semi-Tropic Land and Water Company filed for bankruptcy less than a decade later. Other boosters shared the vision of building an agricultural mecca; they formed the Fontana Development Company in 1901 to keep the irrigation colony alive, and development continued.

Around the turn of the twentieth century, entrepreneur Azariel Blanchard Miller (referred to here and by other sources as A.B.) arrived in the area. The Fontana Development Company leased to the ambitious Miller and three associates the land on which to build. Since Fontana did not consist of much

The land that became the site of Kaiser Steel works, seen here shortly before plant construction began in 1942.

more than a dusty patch, Miller's dream was, kindly put, optimistic. To make Fontana more hospitable to agriculture and "civilized living," Miller ordered thousands of eucalyptus trees planted to provide some kind of vegetation and act as wind breaks. He also ordered that hundreds of miles of concrete pipe be laid for improved distribution of water. In 1910, Miller engaged the Citrus Experiment Station at nearby Riverside, which was attached to the University of California, to jump-start Fontana's citrus production by planting eighty-nine thousand citrus trees. Interestingly, while a handful of Southern California communities that concentrated on citrus cultivation became upscale, Fontana never did. Miller had less desire to attract well-heeled buyers; instead, he targeted more small-scale, self-sufficient, middle-class farmers with modest habits, to carve out an identity for the community.

Among the citrus trees and vineyards, the City of Fontana celebrated its dedication in 1913. Growth came to Fontana, but slowly. Ads taken out in publications tried to lure new settlers to "Fontana Farms" for an idyllic life of growing citrus or walnuts, and maybe raising a few small animals, on parcels with attractive purchase prices (starting at $300–$500). Chickens and rabbits proved popular in Fontana's early days. In the 1920s, pigs became common; within a few years, the town claimed to have the largest

The site of the future Kaiser plant.

hog ranch in the world, the Wade Hog Farm. The popularity of raising pigs led to an unexpected and decidedly unromantic departure from A.B. Miller's vision when, in 1922, the city of Los Angeles signed a ten-year deal with Fontana Farms to export its municipal garbage to Fontana hog farms. Agriculture, in various forms, continued to dominate Fontana's development. Its status as a planned agricultural community was shared with a handful of other Southern California towns—Pasadena, Claremont and Redlands are examples—but Fontana was different. With only seven thousand people living there in 1938, Fontana had a smaller population than those other planned "ag cities." And Fontana developed a grittier and rougher character than them, too.

FONTANA'S SECOND MAJOR CAPITALIST, HENRY J. KAISER, ARRIVES

As the dark clouds of the Great Depression began to finally recede in the closing years of the 1930s, they were replaced by the dark clouds of war. While most Americans wanted to stay clear of this spreading terror,

President Franklin Roosevelt began to prepare the nation for war as much as he could, politically. So the Japanese attack on American military personnel and assets in Hawaii on December 7, 1941, was a surprise, but it did not come completely out of the blue; FDR asked for a declaration of war against Japan the following day. Germany and Italy, Japan's allies, backed up their partner by declaring war on the United States just days after the Pearl Harbor attack. This meant that America would be involved in total war, needing to mobilize every business, farm and person.

Just three months into America's participation in the Second World War, residents in the Fontana area unexpectedly had the war brought right to their doorsteps. On March 5, 1942, the *San Bernardino Sun* announced in a bold print headline, "Valley Site Selected for $50,000,000 Steel Mill." U.S. congressman Harry R. Sheppard telephoned the hot story to *Sun* reporters from his office in Washington, D.C. Sheppard did not reveal the exact location of the future steel plant, but he noted that it would employ five hundred men, produce 450,000 tons of pig iron per year and be operated by "Henry J. Kaiser, Oakland construction engineer and member of the famous Big Six companies of Boulder dam fame." Kaiser's reputation as a builder of heroic-sized projects had already taken off by 1942. The congressman claimed to have gotten federal officials to investigate iron ore reserves at Eagle Mountain in eastern Riverside County, a move he knew would "force the steel industry to develop iron resources of California." None of the federal or company records consulted for this study mentioned Sheppard, so it's possible he played a nominal role, at best, in bringing Kaiser Steel to Fontana.

Beginning with the *Sun*'s March 1942 account, a popular perception grew that Henry Kaiser responded to the nation's wartime need for steel by demanding that he be allowed to build a fully integrated steelworks (which would take ore and convert it into steel products at one site) in California. While it is certainly true that World War II created a sudden and tremendous demand for steel and steel production on the West Coast, which Kaiser sought to satisfy, there is more to the story than one man's desire to make wartime steel following the Japanese attack on Pearl Harbor.

The two biographies written on Henry Kaiser each shed some light on the story behind the origins of the Fontana steelworks. Al Heiner, Henry Kaiser's longtime public relations man and biographer, pointed out, "As early as October 4, 1940, Kaiser submitted his first proposal to the government for the construction of an iron and steel mill on the Pacific Coast, and requested government aid for the project." Mark Foster, Kaiser's other biographer, argued in his book that Kaiser's repeated public calls for more ship plate before 1942 were "camouflage" for his ultimate objective of building his own steel plant. Foster stated that "three months before he signed contracts with the British to construct ships [in 1939], Kaiser envisioned his own fully integrated steel empire in the West." Actually, there are plenty of records that show Kaiser tried to enter steelmaking before he launched his first ship.

Henry Kaiser's meteoric career in business is marked by restlessness; he was always looking to expand. Day-to-day operations bored him, but launching a new enterprise or project excited him, and this is where he spent most of his time. Kaiser began his business career with municipal road construction in 1914 and, from there, pushed his firm into larger and larger construction projects. Within a couple of decades, he became a recognized major player in western construction, participating in some of the West's major water-related construction projects, like the Shasta, Hoover, and Bonneville dams. By the late 1930s, Kaiser appeared ready to move his company from construction to production.

Jack Ashby, who managed the steel operation (from Oakland) for years, told an audience in 1953 that "1937 was the year in which Henry Kaiser concluded in his own mind that a fully integrated steel plant for this West Coast was inevitable and that he should begin taking steps toward the day when it could be established." Kaiser did not have Fontana specifically in mind at that early date, however; Ashby added that "in 1937 Henry Kaiser was dreaming of a steel plant to be located on the water in Southern California." Even then, Kaiser the builder appreciated the traditional logic that dictated steel plants be built adjoining deep water to address the massive transportation costs of moving mountains of raw materials and heavy final product, not to mention satisfy steelmaking's prodigious water consumption. And an integrated steel plant, one that takes raw materials and produces finished steel products at one site, would be able to take full advantage of regional growth because integrated mills tended to be larger than nonintegrated mills, have more extensive product lines and sell bigger steel products, like girders and large-diameter pipes. Kaiser could get in on the ground floor of projected regional growth by building an integrated operation.

The year 1937 was one of some significance for industrialist Kaiser and the American West, his base of operations. In that year, Kaiser had recently completed participating in his most ambitious building project to date, Boulder (Hoover) Dam; Kaiser Company was a member of the Six Companies consortium that built the dam. None of his partners wanted to follow him

President Roosevelt. But despite FDR's fondness for West Coast–made steel, contrary and more cautious opinions in the administration prevailed; memories of the industry running at just 25 percent capacity were fresh. Blocked by opposition, Henry Kaiser did not relent.

While Henry Kaiser assaulted Washington with a barrage of phone calls, letters, telegrams and personal visits, demanding that more steel be delivered to his new shipyards and he be allowed to enter steelmaking, his lieutenants laid down supporting firepower of their own. If the federal approval Kaiser sought could have been gained by sheer tenacity alone, by early 1941, Kaiser would have surely won government approval.

Kaiser tried again to crack this dug-in resistance with a more thorough request submitted to the Office of Production Management (OPM), another powerful government agency, on April 28, 1941. This time, Kaiser first softened up the opposition, making personal visits to high-ranking government men and sending his lieutenants to knock on doors, too. Kaiser needed a "certificate of necessity" from the OPM to obtain controlled material like structural steel and fire brick. Kaiser was preaching to the choir conversing with FDR, but OPM official Edward Stettinius seemed unmovable. It was not unusual for Roosevelt's New Deal and wartime regulatory agencies to have leading businessmen manage them. Stettinius had served as the chairman of the board of U.S. Steel, an unfortunate relationship for Henry Kaiser. Therefore, Stettinius's response that existing steel companies could adequately address the nation's present and future steel needs hardly came as a shock. Kaiser's proposal failed to win OPM approval. But government officials didn't leave Kaiser in the dark, and OPM officers wrote a memorandum to FDR in May 1941 explaining that their rejection was driven mostly by Kaiser's inability to confirm sources for raw materials.

The scope and complexity of Kaiser's second submitted plan is telling. In that application, Kaiser requested permission to build facilities that would make ship plate, but the ambitious Kaiser Company offered not one but five alternative programs for making steel. The proposal did not indicate if Kaiser engineers favored any one of the five options presented, and none of them were in Fontana. Kaiser speculated that the approved plant, which he would own and operate, would need $150 million in funding, with the loan money coming from the Reconstruction Finance Corporation. In all five of the proposed programs, Kaiser wanted the final step in steel production to be located near a key metropolitan area: San Francisco, Los Angeles or Seattle. Among this proposal's more surprising aspects, given Kaiser's oft-stated objective of building a steel plant for providing ship plate, was the request for the capability to produce alloy steels. Alloys found applications outside of simple steel plate, sheet and structural shapes and would have given Kaiser Company the ability to make specialty steels for machining, gears, surgical equipment, aircraft and other highly technical applications. An open-hearth furnace or an old Bessemer converter was all Kaiser needed to produce ship plate. Government officials did not feel sufficiently moved by Kaiser's zeal to overcome their intrinsic cautiousness, and Kaiser received another rejection. Never one to succumb quickly to adversity, and as a measure of his confidence (or perhaps hubris), the industrialist incorporated the Kaiser Company, Iron and Steel Division in Oakland, California, Kaiser's base of operations, on December 1, 1941, six days before the Pearl Harbor attack. On paper, Kaiser Company had entered the steel business.

In Washington, Kaiser kept running up against a brick wall of key people in critical government offices, many of whom were former steel industry men. FDR was never a slave to his advisors, which—along with his long-term interest in expanding the steel industry, piqued by Henry Kaiser—led him to commissioning Gano Dunn to explore expanding steel production. Dunn was also a former advisor to U.S. Steel. Dunn submitted his first analysis to FDR on February 22, 1941, just a month before Kaiser entered his second bid. In short, Dunn concluded that the nation's steel companies possessed plenty of steelmaking capacity, even in a dangerous global environment. Surprisingly, perhaps, Dunn's highly anticipated second report, dated May 22, 1941, reached conclusions diametrically opposed to those provided in his first report. In that three-month span, Dunn had suddenly discovered that "the surpluses of capacity shown in my first report have been turned to deficits." Couched in Dunn's second report is a seemingly compelling reason for his swift change of heart. William A. Hauck, who Dunn mentioned by name in his second report, served as consultant for the Iron and Steel Unit of the Office of Production Management and made a tour of the Pacific Coast in March 1941. His tour and subsequent report got wide attention and offered the newsworthy suggestion that western steel production capacity be boosted by over one million tons. Hauck identified the chief recipient of steel plate as western shipbuilding; West Coast steel production should expand, "and promptly." With Hauck's tour receiving so much attention, Dunn had no choice but to acknowledge him. By the fall of 1941, with more voices calling for change, the OPM announced authorization to expand steelmaking capacity nationwide by ten million tons, with West Coast steel expansion receiving special attention.

What finally removed the last roadblocks to Kaiser joining the ranks of America's steelmakers was the Japanese attack on Pearl Harbor on December 7, 1941. Vastly increased steel production from coast to coast would be needed—and fast. No longer could requests for permission and funding by Kaiser, the Depression's "can-do capitalist," be easily turned aside. The time was ripe for another Kaiser assault on Washington.

In December 1941, Kaiser and his lieutenants peppered Washington bureaucrats with urgent requests. Using novel techniques such as mass-production-like assembly, widespread welding and employing female workers, Kaiser shipyards in the Pacific Northwest and San Francisco Bay had been launching ships for several months (Portland's first ship set sail in May 1941), and crews were producing an increasing number of ships, in an amazingly shorter time than hitherto seen in traditional shipbuilding—from months to just days. Cranking out ships, Kaiser complained of steel shortages at his yards and the reluctance or inability of established steel firms to fill promised orders. Seemingly overnight, Kaiser had graduated from being a noisy outsider clamoring for entry to a legitimate steel consumer with national security implications. In a letter to OPM assistant director A.I. Henderson dated December 24, Christmas Eve, Kaiser warned that without more steel, "it now appears that there is a possibility that we will have idle shipbuilding facilities in California, while the enemy is sinking ships off the California coast." He directly asked Henderson, "Is it too late to start construction of additional steel facilities for supplying West Coast needs?" Kaiser posed another pointed question to Henderson: "Now that we are faced with an actual war" and "existing steel companies are already failing to meet the minimum requirements for shipbuilding, how can we expect to further augment the shipbuilding operation?" That same day, Kaiser also sent a copy of this letter to William Hauck, along with a short note that concluded with Kaiser asking Hauck abruptly, "What will you do?" Moved to hear Kaiser out, Hauck asked to meet with the pushy shipbuilder in February 1942. Kaiser now had his foot in the door. The first offer the government made limited Kaiser's metal making to pig iron only, not steel, and it would primarily be sent to East Coast plants to finish. The government would cover the costs of building the plant through the DPC, leaving Kaiser Company to operate it. This was not at all what Kaiser wanted, and he rejected the plan.

Even after the Pearl Harbor attack, many high-ranking government officials remained opposed to Kaiser's steel expansion plans. So OPM's William Hauck tried to smooth Kaiser's ruffled feathers by lauding him: "As we all know, you are contributing very strongly to the defense effort in your various shipyards, magnesium plant, and other industries." And Hauck kept the door open by writing, "We will appreciate any further ideas that you think would be of additional help on the West Coast steel supply." While in Washington in February 1942, Kaiser decided to keep knocking on doors until he found the answers he wanted. The Defense Plant Corporation remained reluctant to fund the construction of the kind of steel plant Kaiser wanted. William Allen of the DPC told Kaiser that under no circumstances would he approve the spending of one dime of government money for any blast furnace in California.

Still, Kaiser sensed some weakening of resistance, so he shifted the target of his attack to Sam Husbands and Jesse Jones of the Reconstruction Finance Corporation (RFC) for possible funding. If the RFC handled the funding for Kaiser's steelworks, the government would loan Kaiser the money to build the plant, then Kaiser would own and operate it. Kaiser informed RFC officials that the Maritime Commission had requested him to build three more shipyards on the West Coast, plus more ships. He impressed upon them the ongoing shortage of steel at his yards and the delays in production that this caused. And he berated figures outside government as well. Ben Fairless, president of U.S. Steel, the giant in American steel production, found himself the unlucky recipient of Kaiser's considerable vitriol. "You should know," Kaiser bluntly asserted in a letter dated June 30, 1941, "that your companies have unqualifiedly failed in their promise of deliveries." Kaiser then rattled off a handful of ships under construction at his yards whose completion was delayed up to several weeks because of the missing steel shapes and plate, using the uncomfortably direct phrase "you should know" over ten times. "You should know," he continued, "that it is fatal to America's future if you do not immediately correct the situation which causes the above conditions." Although Kaiser curtly apologized for taking that tone with Fairless, he gave one of America's leading businessmen a dressing-down that lasted for two full single-spaced typed pages. He sent an almost identical letter to Eugene Grace, president of Bethlehem Steel, America's number two steelmaker, that same day. Duly convinced of Kaiser's needs, and perhaps fearing a similar tongue-lashing, Sam Husbands of the RFC acquiesced to Kaiser's demands, agreeing to loan sufficient money to build a plant to Kaiser's specifications, if he could: (1) get a letter from WPB leaders stating that the project was a necessity of war, (2) secure a certificate of war necessity from the WPB that would give the Kaiser plant a high priority for materials and men, and (3) present satisfactory evidence of shipbuilding contracts. Clearly, there was positive movement in Kaiser's direction.

Now the dogged industrialist fine-tuned his request. On February 24, 1942, officials from the WPB agreed that a new blast furnace was essential to the war effort and wrote a letter to that effect, granting a certificate of necessity to Kaiser Company that could then be presented to the Reconstruction Finance Corporation. Armed with a certificate of necessity from the WPB and ship orders from the Maritime Commission, Kaiser revisited RFC officials and received a funding promise in the form of loans; he had cleared the last of the hurdles put in front of him. The multimillion-dollar loan (which ultimately rose to a total of $123,305,000) made to Kaiser won approval only after he agreed to pledge profits from three of his shipyards to cover loan payments. Thus, technically, even though Kaiser Company could claim that it owned the plant, the federal government held the note on the operation. Therefore, if the steel operation failed, even after Kaiser had begun making loan payments, the government would assume ownership. These were terms acceptable to Henry Kaiser, a price he was willing to pay to break into the steel business. This was big news indeed, and it grabbed the attention of the national media. For example, *Business Week* said that the government approval "revives Kaiser's ambition to establish an independent 'steel empire' on the West Coast."

But Kaiser did not get something for nothing from the government in 1942. For example, his critics—and he had plenty—failed to acknowledge that the government still held the note on the plant. He had to repay those loans in full, plus interest. And he continued to haggle with bureaucrats during and after the war over the conditions of the loan and its repayment. Henry Kaiser did not always get his way with the federal government, and any criticism that he steamrolled over the government is misplaced.

Kaiser not getting his way with the government is nowhere better illustrated than when it came to where the government allowed him to build. After obtaining permission and funding, where to build the plant had to be determined. By the time Kaiser got his permission, Southern California remained the only area where he wanted to build. Broadly speaking, this met with government approval; Southern California was not an issue per se. A memorandum from within Kaiser Company written in early February 1942 listed eight Southern California sites that had been under active consideration by the company. A few of these eight no longer had support from Kaiser's engineers, though. Already out of the running by this point was a site near the Long Beach airport, which was terrifically expensive at $1,300 per acre. Difficult topography and existing infrastructure also knocked the Union Oil terminal in Los Angeles out of the running. Getting the most attention in the memo was Port Hueneme (which the report misspelled as Huenene); according to Al Heiner, "Right down to the end of the negotiations, Kaiser kept insisting that his plant be located at Port Hueneme." Kaiser's preference for that location recognized the accepted economics of efficient steel plant operation, which dictated proximity to abundant water, plus the steady history of population growth Southern California had witnessed.

But for as much as sense as Port Hueneme made to Kaiser Company accountants and engineers, Washington bureaucrats worried about the ability of the Japanese to lob shells onto the new facility or attack cargo ships serving it. Heiner observed that "the government flatly ruled it out." Instead, the government representatives countered that Barstow, California, some 125 miles inland in the desert, would be acceptable. It is worth remembering that the Japanese military did in fact shell the coast north of Los Angeles in February 1942, doing little physical damage but terrifying millions. This was not their only attack on the continental United States, either. And it needs to be pointed out that the federal government also nixed Bethlehem Steel's proposal, proffered shortly before war broke out, to build a fully integrated steelworks in Los Angeles.

Then there was Fontana. The location of Fontana has remained controversial throughout the plant's history. It was one of those eight sites in the February 1942 Kaiser Company memo, so it was a site the company had investigated and considered. A decade after the plant was approved, Jack Ashby told a group of businessmen in San Francisco that "we chose Fontana as the location primarily because of its proximity to Los Angeles.... We had to be realistic in recognizing that Los Angeles is the largest steel-consuming market in the West." With Barstow unattractive to Kaiser and Port Hueneme unattractive to the government, Fontana was a compromise both sides could live with.

Fontana was not Kaiser's first choice for locating an integrated steelworks, but it boasted of having several elements that made it attractive. Its proximity to Los Angeles meant useful infrastructure was in place: rail lines and multiple developed roads. Iron ore and limestone could be found relatively close by Fontana and transported by rail to the plant. There was plenty of room to build in Fontana, too. Kaiser gave his people the command to "think big, don't allow operations to be cramped," and in Fontana, large blocks of land could be purchased cheap. And technically, the Kaiser plant did not locate in the city of Fontana proper; it was instead in unincorporated area of San Bernardino County, even after Fontana incorporated in 1952. San Bernardino County had a plentiful labor supply, and then again, Los Angeles

the steelworks would damage their trees. Apparently, she and others realized that it would be futile battling against the war effort, local boosters and the powerful Kaiser Company. Luksich concluded, "We didn't have the money to do one thing about it." Minnie Luksich, realizing, like many other growers in the area, the profound transition Fontana faced, stood down and, in her case, eventually obtained a job at the Kaiser steelworks. By granting Kaiser Company approval to build, the county board began to close the door on the agricultural phase of Fontana's history and open another.

Chapter 2

WORLD WAR II AND KAISER STEEL'S FONTANA "LOVE CHILD"

B y the late 1930s, Henry Kaiser had begun to emerge as a "seer" of sorts, and he received increasing attention in the media for his forecasting a near future where exciting new technology would change the lives of ordinary Americans, things like "$400 postwar autos, [personal] helicopters, prefabricated houses and mass produced medical care." In his career, he had accomplished seemingly impossible feats, so why not believe him here? In the years around 1940, it appeared this dreamer of an industrialist had the wind at his back and the proposition that he enter steelmaking might become a reality.

HENRY KAISER BUILDS A STEEL PLANT

True to form, Henry J. Kaiser approached building the Fontana steelworks as he did many of his other projects—as one of his biographers described it, "by the seat of his pants." In mid-February 1942, with government approval for a steel mill in hand, Kaiser contacted his chief engineer, George Havas, and matter-of-factly stated, "George, you're going to build me a steel mill." Familiar with his boss's unpredictable requests, Havas calmly replied, "What kind of a steel mill?" "Oh, just a steel mill," Kaiser countered, "a small one." Henry J. had no idea how to build a steel plant and could not have cared less, but he knew Havas could either do it or figure out how to do it. Kaiser dreamed the big dreams in this company, lined up the cash and addressed

The heart of Kaiser Steel's Fontana operation was its first blast furnace, "the Bess," shown here in 1942.

some other major issues, then left the details of assembling and operating his dreams to a cadre of young lieutenants, allowing him to take off to his next big project. Fontana was no exception. Havas, joined by Chad Calhoun and Tom Price, engineered and built the steelmaking facility. Kaiser's trusted son Edgar was busy building ships at the time but occasionally helped with the Fontana project in its early days. Edgar Kaiser exerted a much more influential role in the company's operation in the postwar period. Henry Kaiser Jr. occupied a secondary role, as he lacked the family's trademark hard-charging nature and was slowed by health problems diagnosed later as multiple sclerosis.

With the war raging in the spring of 1942 and much steel needing to be made immediately, the Fontana steel plant seemed to spring up overnight. Tom Price, Kaiser's trusted employee since 1919, flew up from Panama in March 1942 to oversee plant construction as works manager. Price got right to work securing land; Kaiser Company paid over $250,000 to owners to secure the title to their property. Bulldozers broke ground on April 13, 1942, about two weeks after county supervisors granted permission to build. The machines bulldozed the land free of buildings and vegetation, literally pushing pigs from their longtime homes with no fanfare. "This is war," declared Price. "We are too busy for ceremonies or celebrations, all we have time for is work and more work!" Kaiser engineers, who some eastern engineers called Kaiser's "orange juice boys," "sunshine boys" or "cement dusters," purchased some new equipment from swamped suppliers but oftentimes had to settle for used, inadequate and dated machinery. Some critical pieces could not be purchased at any price and had to be fabricated on the spot. A good example of this problem occurred when Kaiser Company tried to purchase open hearth ladle stands with no success. Havas said, "We finally designed them ourselves and had them fabricated from some used 36" beams which had been a part of the concrete placing trestle at Grand Coulee Dam." Even the famous Kaiser optimism and energy had limits on what could be done without help, and Kaiser obtained assistance from established steel firms; patriotism trumped competition in the early 1940s. Kaiser engineers traveled to eastern steel plants to witness the operation of different types of blast furnaces and picked the exact design used at a Republic Steel plant as the model; one business publication at the time opined that "without

Construction of the Fontana plant continued around the clock, as seen in this night photo, 1942.

Kaiser's undeveloped Vulcan iron mine in 1942; the darker soil with iron ore is evident.

that assistance, Kaiser probably would not have erected his steel mill." Kaiser Company hired a number of outside construction outfits to help in-house talent build the plant, including Consolidated Steel Corporation and Bethlehem Steel, both of Los Angeles, and Bechtel-McCone-Parsons (Bechtel had teamed up with Kaiser to build Hoover Dam and the Pacific Northwest shipyards). Building raced forward, with Price recalling that "innumerable times, plans still wet from the blueprinters were rushed down by air (from Oakland) to keep the construction crews going."

Another hurdle (or opportunity, as Henry would say) the plant faced was obtaining sufficient raw materials at a good cost. Henry Kaiser had argued that Southern California made a sensible choice for locating a mine-to-metal steel facility in part because of the plentiful raw materials in the region, but actually delivering on that claim proved difficult. Kaiser engineers had already done some preliminary scouting for essential steelmaking ingredients, but much of the information in their reports was speculative, sometimes even wildly optimistic. A key ingredient, iron ore, did exist in appreciable amounts in Southern California. All this ore was landlocked, though, and ore is often moved by water to save money. Fontana would have to use rail and, even less attractively, truck transportation to move gigantic amounts of ore. Of great interest to Kaiser engineers were the confirmed huge iron ore deposits at Eagle Mountain, about 150 miles east of Fontana in a rugged portion of Riverside County. Preliminary geological reports suggested that "the total tonnage is large and probably sufficient to support any probable operation in this region but the mining costs will be relatively high." Unfortunately for Kaiser Company, this attractive ore source locked up its iron below considerable "overburden": dirt and rocks on top. Plus, the sheer remoteness and lack of development of the area necessitated sizable capital investment and time to build facilities. Finally, several parties contested ownership of the mine. The costs and logistics of making Eagle Mountain operational stood in the way of its immediate use by Kaiser. Several other sites emerged as possible stopgap solutions. With its easily recovered ore, short distance to a major rail line and motivated owner with clear title, Vulcan Mine won the day. Located about 180 miles east of Fontana, near Kelso, the undeveloped area did not look like much from a cursory visual inspection. Expecting to find an impressive mountain of iron, an "incredulous" Tom Price declared it nothing more than "a small dark spot on a hill about 100 ft. in diameter." In fact, the next day he asked Henry Kaiser if he was "crazy to build a plant like that with no more ore in sight than Vulcan promised." Kaiser Company nonetheless quickly purchased the mine. Modest-sized reserves, high sulfur content and an expensive nine-mile truck haul down steep 7 percent grades to the railhead doomed it to a brief production stint. Still, the Vulcan Mine yielded over 2.5 million tons of ore for Kaiser Company over its roughly six years of operation as Fontana's chief source for stoking its blast furnaces. If Kaiser meant to stay in steelmaking only for the duration of the war, Vulcan would have been sufficient to satisfy Fontana's demand for ore.

A second basic ingredient used in the blast furnace, limestone, could also be easily found in Southern California. Limestone was widely available and cheap, as well as used in several industries, like concrete. Kaiser Company purchased it off the market through the war; Kaiser later purchased its own limestone mine in Cushenbury, California, about seventy-five miles from Fontana in the Lucerne Valley.

Locating an attractive source for the third essential blast furnace ingredient, coking coal, however, proved to be a persistent headache for Kaiser engineers and accountants. Significant California reserves of coking coal, which is coal that can be baked to make coke, were simply not available in Fontana's immediate vicinity. Coke makes a superior ingredient for blast furnaces, which reduce iron ore to molten iron, and not just any coal will do.

Loading ore at Vulcan mine, 1943; it was not a major mining operation.

Kaiser needed worker accommodations in a hurry that would only be used for a few years; housing at the Vulcan mine was modest.

Certain types of coal can be "coked," literally baked, to drive off volatile substances and water to create coke. The Fontana plant would consume over one million tons of coke per year, so not being able to rely on a site that could provide enough cheaply obtained coking coal posed a project-killing problem. In fact, Kaiser had to look very far afield to find an adequate source for this mineral. In April 1942, Henry Kaiser called Moroni Heiner, president of the Utah Fuel Company, about buying coal from their massive Sunnyside mine in eastern Utah. Kaiser expressed his desire to purchase the mine; he believed that he could slash labor costs with new machinery and mitigate the costs of the long haul to Fontana. Henry J. and his lieutenants virtually ganged up on Moroni, but he only agreed to sell coal to Kaiser. Kaiser Company obtained coal from many sources over the years, then in fact later purchased the Sunnyside mine, but Kaiser never found an ideal source of coking coal close to Fontana.

Hiring enough workers, particularly ones skilled in working with hot metal made from ore, tested the inventiveness of Henry Kaiser and his aides as much as obtaining ore did. With about fifteen million Americans putting on uniforms in World War II, the Fontana plant was not the only defense plant facing a shortage of workers. The West Coast labor market tightened up after years of chronic unemployment; however, electricians, machinists, welders and other industrial workers could be obtained locally. Operating a crane, whether on a seaside dock or in a steel plant, was fundamentally the same procedure. But unfortunately for Kaiser Company, there were many skills needed in mine-to-metal steelmaking not transferable from other industries, like separating the waste slag from molten iron in a blast furnace. Simply put, Kaiser had to assemble a small core of trained steelworkers to fill those positions unique to steelmaking. And California's pool of available steelworkers, who worked in "melt shops" and rolling mills, did not meet that need. These mills did not have great numbers of excess workers, as California employed over ten thousand steelworkers at the time, and their employers also faced a worker shortage once wartime mobilization began— plus they had no experience with molten metal. "Making a product like steel," recalled former Kaiser steelworker John Piazza, "it has to kind of be in your system. You have to grow up around it, have a feeling for it." Piazza grew up in Pennsylvania and came west to work at the Fontana steelworks in the 1940s. Piazza had a grandfather, uncles and other family members in steel. Kaiser employee Vern Maxie pointed out that safety was an issue: "When they started up the mill and you get the hot molten metal, and pouring from the open hearth and blast furnace…soaking pits, and plate mill," it was no

There is a great amount of intricate masonry used in integrated steel plants, like in and around the Bess, shown here under construction.

place for on-the-job training. Simply put, if Kaiser Company was going to make any steel before the war ended, it would first have to import some skilled steelworkers and steel mill managers from eastern plants.

Kaiser fell back on a novel source of help to find that nucleus of trained workers for Fontana: organized labor. Recognizing the potential for job creation that Fontana promised, many of them good-paying union jobs, and the uphill struggle this operation faced, national labor leaders stood solidly behind Kaiser to help him build and staff his plant. The United Steelworkers of America (USWA) union, led by Phil Murray, personally approved Kaiser Company to troll in eastern waters for card-carrying union steelworkers to hire and move out west. A former high-ranking United Steelworkers official in Southern California, Cass Alvin, recalled that Murray helped coordinate the search for the right mix of skilled workers, "but in sort of a clandestine way." Alvin continued, "What we did then, is we encouraged people to come to Kaiser in Fontana." Union representatives traveled to steel plants represented by the USWA and asked workers with certain skills if they would consider moving to the West Coast. Not surprisingly, recruiters often spoke of the balmy weather, the movie stars and other widely recognized examples of Southern California imagery to woo workers. It proved to be a pretty easy sell. Records of just how many workers made the migration west to work for Fontana no longer remain, but it was likely several hundred.

Rivaling the difficulty Kaiser management had with filling their labor needs was the challenge of finding places for these workers to live. The largely rural area of Fontana had only a limited number of houses or apartments to rent or buy. Since the surrounding San Bernardino Valley also attracted new military and working families to the area during the war, Kaiser Company workers faced considerable competition for housing. Kaiser's first construction workers snapped up the small supply of empty houses and rooms in the immediate area, leading to the common and unfortunate practice of Kaiser workers living in cars, sheds, chicken coops and other substandard accommodations for several years. Driving from other communities farther away was unattractive because the war brought both an end to passenger car production and the advent of tire and gasoline rationing. The company responded to housing needs in a variety of ways. As early as 1942, workers could sign up for living in two company-owned trailer courts. Residents christened the courts "Kaiserville," and the comings and goings of the area became a regular feature of Kaiser Company, Iron and Steel Division's paper, the *Snorter*. Additionally, there is photographic evidence of a small cluster of flat-roofed dwellings referred to as a "shantytown," right on the plant grounds. The Federal Housing Authority worked with Kaiser Company to build small and simple single-family dwellings for workers

HOMES LIKE THIS have sheltered many Kaiser workmen and their families since construction first started. This is Mrs. Gale G. Wilson at her front door. He is a superintendent at the open hearth furnace and was the first to bring a trailer to Kaiserville.

Some of the makeshift Fontana-area housing highlighted in the *Snorter*, the company's first newspaper.

The company paper covering the blowing-in of the Bess; this was the first issue of the *Snorter*.

only a seven-minute drive from the plant. Qualified workers could move into them beginning in early 1943, and the area became informally referred to as "Fontana Plaza." For Fontana's few African American workers, who held mostly low-status jobs as common laborers and materials handlers, the company built separate structures. While not under the influence of a well-defined set of Jim Crow Laws, Southern California's growing Black population nonetheless faced segregation in housing. Kaiser Company responded to the housing needs of these (single) African American male workers and bowed to the prevailing racial mores by building separate small, darkly colored buildings shaped like inverted bathtubs, called "igloos." Four men squeezed into each, although the shacks were only about ten feet tall and ten feet wide at the base. The igloos lacked cooling, toilets and kitchens; instead, the men used a "central wash house and comfort station." Living in these quarters, which were located on the plant site, freed Black employees from worrying about commuting to work, but these huts must have been miserable living spaces.

Through these various means, Kaiser Company quickly staffed several thousand open positions at the new plant, in spite of the wartime labor shortage, and found some kind of roof to put over most of the workers' heads. Employment at the Fontana plant during the war years peaked in 1944 at 3,561 workers.

Fontana Commences Production

After only nine months of frantic planning, building and securing men and materials, the Fontana steelworks began limited metal production, an amazing accomplishment; "Miracle Man" Kaiser had pulled off yet another impossible feat. December 30, 1942, marked the dedication of the plant with the ceremonial "blowing in"—that is to say, igniting—of Fontana's first blast furnace. The blast furnace, which made iron from iron ore (called, in this first step, pig iron), was widely looked upon as the heart of a steel plant, so celebrating the opening of the blast furnace marked the ability of the plant to make metal. The celebration had all of the Southern California trimmings: radio coverage, movie newsreels, motion picture personalities, government and business dignitaries and some five to eight thousand observers (the number varied depending on who did the counting). The media carried the celebration to millions nationwide, with the relatively unknown local media figure Chet Huntley carrying the event for NBC radio. The Reverend John Macdonald of the Fontana Community Church lifted up a prayer: "We thank Thee O God, for men who have the courage to dream, and to make their dreams come true; for those who make the desert bloom with the plants of industry; for the skilled craftsmen who weave their webs of steel; for the artisan and the army of toilers who, blending their skill with their strength, will enable us to redeem the promise to our fighting forces and our brave allies, to supply them with the tools of war to complete the task for which we are all committed." In his address to the crowd, Henry Kaiser further emphasized Fontana's raison d'être to serve the war effort, declaring, "Ships are the greatest need of the hour. The shortage of steel and materials is the only thing that stands in the way of vastly increased production." Patriotic talk and symbols dominated the day.

There was some looking beyond the immediate demands of war, though. Writers for the local *Ontario Daily Report* saw an industrial future in their valley, describing the Fontana steel plant as forging a "new empire link" in a "new and widespread industrial empire of the West," employing "thousands of men when they return from the battlefields." Likewise, Henry Kaiser, while keeping the focus of his words on the war, still noted, "What this event holds in terms of promise for the future is the story on which we would like to dwell if not for the stern requirements of war."

Henry Kaiser Jr. served as master of ceremonies. The platform party included Henry Sr., Henry Jr., Edgar, and their wives. Henry Sr.'s wife, Bess, was presented a "Victory Bouquet" made partially of defense stamps. An entertainer at the gala, Martie Hubble Berhart, remembered that "Bess came in like a gunboat—with that big bosom and those huge flowers." Mrs. Kaiser flipped a switch that simulated a dramatic ignition of the blast furnace. In reality, though, Mrs. Kaiser's switch flip ignited a small quantity of magnesium "goop," a Kaiser Company product made a few hundred miles north and used in incendiary bombs. The switch also simultaneously tripped horns on top of the furnace. A local newspaper account described the afternoon as a "well-staged, well-directed event." Management named Fontana's 1,200-ton capacity blast furnace in Mrs. Kaiser's honor: "the Bess," a structure that became well known in the years ahead. The Bess remained Fontana's only blast furnace throughout the war, continuing on the job until 1983.

Once properly inaugurated at the blowing-in ceremony, the Fontana facility continued to amaze observers. The first steel production came on

Striking a familiar pose, Henry Kaiser addresses a nationwide audience at the dedication of Fontana's first blast furnace in 1942.

The hard-charging H.J. Kaiser at the ceremonial blowing-in of the Bess.

The first push of coke at the Fontana plant, 1943.

May 14, 1943, with Henry Sr. personally giving the order to "tap" the first steel from the plant's open hearth furnaces. This first batch transformed 210 tons of ingredients—molten pig iron produced in the Bess, along with steel scrap, limestone and manganese—into 185 tons of steel. The rest of the product emerging from the open hearth was a waste called "slag," a material of little commercial value (at that time). Henry J.'s command that day steered the molten steel out of the open hearth into a huge ladle, then into forms to cool as ingots. Since Fontana's rolling mills had not yet been finished, the steel was done being processed there. The open hearth furnaces cranked out heats (batches) of steel every nine hours; the ingots produced were shipped to mills across America and as far away as Great Britain.

Beyond making metal, a steel plant usually makes metal into consumer-ready products, usually in some kind of mill. Fontana's rolling mills began to open in 1944. These massive machines, found in buildings oftentimes also called mills, transformed steel ingots into usable shapes and sizes. The rolling mill department, comprising part of what was sometimes called the "finished end" or "back end" of the steelworks, occupied some of the largest structures on the early plant grounds, taking up five hundred thousand square feet of land. These mills accepted massive pieces of hot steel, called ingots, and then rolled and sheared them into the desired shapes. These ingots each weighed several tons and had to be kept at malleable temperatures, around 2,000 degrees Fahrenheit. Great tongs moved the ingots from soaking pits to mill and back. Soaking pits were large furnaces dug into the ground that fired the steel ingots to a malleable heat, fueled in part by fuel oil and in part by waste gases recovered from the blast furnace. The steel traveled through a series of mills until being rolled and sheared to the desired dimensions. The first three major mills in the rolling department opened in quick succession, number one being the plate mill. The plate mill provided a staple product for Fontana plate that could be further rolled into other applications, from pipe to tin can stock. Fontana's plate mill had the primary duty, during the war years, to produce ship plate. Kaiser Company steelworkers produced Fontana's first steel plate on August 19, 1943. Workers rolled the first plate, sheared it to the desired proportions, then loaded it onto a flatbed semitrailer for delivery. The truck sped the steel four hundred miles north to waiting Kaisership workers in Richmond (in northern California near Oakland, where Kaiser Company was headquartered) who fitted it immediately onto the deck of a waiting Liberty Ship under construction, the SS *Robert Moczkowski*. In typical Kaiser shipyard fashion, the ship launched that same day. The demand was certainly there for every bit of plate Fontana rolled. Kaiser's West Coast yards produced some 1,500 craft during the war, an amount totaling about one-third of all cargo ships produced by the United States.

It takes more than steel plate to build a ship, much less grow a diversified industrial base in the American West, and Kaiser Company's steel plant rolled more than ship plate during the war. The second mill to come on line during the war was the structural mill. Opening in 1944, this mill produced shapes such as beams, angles and channels. The plant's merchant mill opened in 1945 to produce various sizes of steel bars. With a capacity of 1.5 million tons of steel per year in 1945, Fontana did not figure as a huge plant by national standards.

Virtually always overlooked in accounts of Kaiser Steel was the plant's brief foray into shell casing manufacture. In the spring of 1944, with about a year left in the war, Kaiser Company won federal approval to build a mill at Fontana to manufacture artillery shell casings. The $25 million facility, at first employing about fifty men, machined steel poured at Fontana into the rough casings for 8-inch and 155-millimeter shells. These were only roughly machined casings, which got loaded onto trains to an ordnance plant in

The first steel plate rolled at Fontana, 1943.

Fontana's short-lived and small electric furnace, 1944.

Denver—a plant, in fact, leased to another Kaiser Company division—which finished machining and assembly.

Evidence of Henry Kaiser's "long game" for Fontana, way beyond serving the war, is easy to find. His requests to add an electric furnace to make steel are a great example. Having such a furnace would allow the plant to make alloy steels more easily. Early in the permit-gaining process, regulators rejected Kaiser's requests to allow him to build an electric furnace, but Kaiser, who hated to hear the word *no*, kept applying pressure. In the summer of 1943, Kaiser engineer Chad Calhoun wrote a letter to Hiland Batcheller, vice-chairman and director of the War Production Board's (WPB) Steel Division, again requesting permission to build an electric furnace. Citing Fontana's remarkably quick start-up time, which he called "characteristic promptness," Calhoun promised that if Kaiser Company was given permission to build and operate an electric furnace, the plant could add one hundred thousand tons to its steelmaking capacity that same year. Here was Henry Kaiser's new, alluring approach: adding an electric furnace would augment the open hearths' steel production. While citing Kaiser's "splendid cooperation" in helping meet urgent steel demand, Batcheller encouraged Kaiser management to concentrate efforts on achieving maximum production with approved facilities, saying, "It is my opinion that you can best serve by concentrating all of your energy and initiative on the early completion" of approved facilities and products. But Kaiser would not be denied. The WPB finally yielded to Kaiser's requests, and the electric furnace expansion at Fontana won approval. Because of the relative ease of setting up this machinery, workers began pouring steel in June 1944. At first, the WPB granted permission to build a tiny ten-ton furnace, but Kaiser Company engineers built one of thirty-ton capacity. Kaiser's record-breaking production earned him the grateful respect of Washington bureaucrats, but they found it difficult to contain Kaiser's ambitions; Secretary of Commerce Jesse Jones felt compelled to remind Henry Kaiser in a telegram, "Keep up the good work but stay on the track."

Water usage was a pretty unique problem Fontana faced, and maximizing use of the precious liquid taxed Kaiser engineers. All water for the Fontana steelworks was purchased from a local water company or pumped from wells on-site. Two separate systems were built: one for human use (called domestic) and one for industrial use. Wastewater from the domestic system passed through a sewage treatment facility, then flowed into the industrial system. The industrial water cooled equipment and materials. All water used on equipment was reclaimed and reused; only a small percentage of industrial water, such as that sprayed to cool coke emerging from the ovens, was lost to evaporation. Engineers constructed large cooling towers, settling tanks and water storage towers to accomplish this. Typical American steel plants in the mid-twentieth century, by design located on deep water, used some 40,000 to 60,000 gallons of water for every ton of steel produced. By stark comparison, the Kaiser works consumed only about 1,400 gallons for every ton of steel used, another remarkable achievement for Kaiser engineers, making it perhaps the most water-efficient steel plant in America.

Just as Kaiser Steel's water usage made Fontana unique among steel plants, so did company concern for airborne vapor and smoke emanating from the plant. Looking back from the vantage point of the twenty-first century, with more than half a century of aggressive local, state and federal regulations of airborne pollutants being such a high-profile matter, it's noteworthy that Kaiser Steel initiated a costly program to mitigate pollution right away, without governmental impetus. Kaiser engineers utilized the most effective means known at the time to control smoke and gases produced. Some smokestacks were made larger than average diameter and taller than average height to carry away the offending substances and odors; the highest stacks at the Fontana plant reached about three hundred feet into the air. According to Kaiser Steel officials, the dispersion of gases into the upper atmosphere was considered an advanced method of disposal. The Bess had gas-cleaning equipment installed on it from the very start. While many parts of the plant emitted some noxious products, the coke ovens presented an especially vexing challenge. The combustion in the coke oven released volatile materials from the coal, so engineers had to devise ways to capture those liberated substances. Innumerable small cracks in the oven's brickwork allowed gases to exit, and when the doors opened to push out the cooked coke, large volumes of gases came along with it. The volatile agents in coke oven gas were a "who's who" of carcinogens and other poisons. That these substances had some deleterious effects to life was known even then, so Kaiser engineers installed self-sealing doors on the ovens and suction fans that attempted to contain the agents released. The gases made their way through a series of precipitators, coolers, distillers and other means to isolate parts of the oven gas, along with light oils, tar and pitch. Environmental concern (keeping neighbors happy) was a driver for company engineers, but there was money in these waste products, too. Kaiser Company sold some of the isolated substances from the coke ovens to processing plants for use in the rubber, petroleum, pharmaceutical, paint and explosive industries. The wartime applications of these valuable materials added considerably to Fontana's worth in supporting the war effort. What remained in coke oven gas after removing the volatiles was still quite high in energy content, so it was routed by pipes around the plant for use as a fuel in the soaking pits and other combustion applications. Unfortunately, however, Kaiser's open hearth furnaces operated without any pollution control, releasing their emissions into the atmosphere unchecked, and these emissions were highly visible, foul smelling and dangerous. Steelmaking is an inherently dirty process, and Kaiser engineers applied the best technology available to mitigate the plant's impact.

The company's *Snorter* newspaper worked on marrying industry with agriculture through more subtle means. One conspicuous way was an illustration seen for several years at the top of page one of every issue of the *Snorter*. Nestled behind the flora in the foreground, complete with regular rows of trees looking very much like a citrus orchard, stood Kaiser's benign factory. Flanking the citrus trees in the foreground, a tractor tilled a field, with "KCI" (as the paper often referred to the company) on its side.

The Snorter reported the efforts of workers trying their hand at agriculture at the steelworks with pictures and articles that had titles like "Power

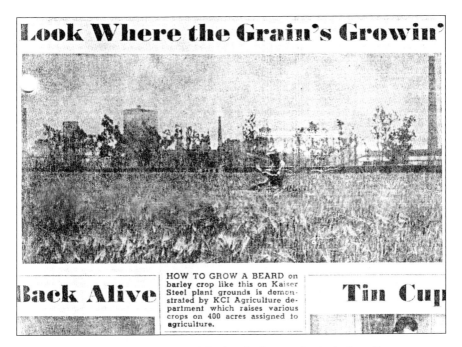

An article in the company's postwar publication the *Ingot* on the Agriculture Department maintaining crops around the steelworks in the 1940s.

House Employe [sic] Plants Victory Garden as Tribute to Family Left Home in Poland" and "Boys at Sewage Plant Grow Prosperous Garden on the Side." Kaiser's facility might have been the only one in America that boasted of having manicured lawns, flowers, fields under cultivation and palm trees. Kaiser Company's efforts to make its Fontana plant look different from other steel facilities grabbed the attention of *Architectural Forum*, which published an extensive photographic study of the steel mill in a 1944 issue. The article claimed that "Kaiser's plant would win hands down in any beauty contest for steel mills." The *Christian Science Monitor* went so far as to write that a "Country Club Aura Surrounds Kaiser's Fontana Steel Plant." One Pennsylvania-born Kaiser worker, Ginny Mulloy, used to bring visiting steelworker family to her place of work. "That's one thing when my relatives came out and we took them they would notice," she recalled years later. "There were live plants!"

Unfortunately, Kaiser Company engineers miscalculated the deleterious effects the plant would have on local agriculture. "All Fontana was groves at that time. The fumes from the mill steeled in a low spot where our property was and it injured our trees; we didn't get the crops we once did," local farmer Minnie Luksich remembered. To address the concerns of agriculturalists, Kaiser Company retained the services of citrus experts and plant pathologists to monitor effects of the steelworks on the environment. Kaiser's Agriculture Department cultivated hundreds of acres of land for years. But despite the efforts of Kaiser engineers to minimize the negative impact of steelmaking on the environment, Fontana's production brought a pall over Fontana's once thriving agriculture, helping end Fontana's romantic, rural way of life.

Supporters of San Bernardino County agriculture had little power to stop the Kaiser plant from coming, and they found little assistance or sympathy among local legislators when they complained of the plant's emissions once the plant began to impact production. Evidence of a rift between agricultural interests and Kaiser Company can be detected in the struggle over determining the steel plant's county tax bill. In July 1943, Henry J. Kaiser traveled to San Bernardino to speak to the county board of supervisors to convince them to lower the mill's tax assessment by several million dollars. Kaiser claimed "we cannot survive" unless some adjustment to valuation was made. There is no explicit mention of opposition voiced by specific farmers or farm groups at this meeting, but Kaiser did obliquely acknowledge the existence of people "who are opposed to the industrialization of this county." Kaiser then assured the board that Fontana would not turn into another Pittsburgh, saying, "You don't need to lose what has been lost in other steel centers, such as flowers, trees, and all things that make it a living garden....[Our plant] is more like a campus than a steel plant." Kaiser's efforts paid off handsomely, as the board settled on a valuation of the Fontana plant of just $8.7 million, trimming the figure about $3 million. Kaiser Company received the assessment revaluation in 1943 and the following year. When the mill received its county tax bill and taxes, Henry J. had to repeat his performance before the county board. This second time, however, opposition to Kaiser's special treatment resisted with vocal dissent. *Business Week* magazine reported in 1944 that "agricultural interests in San Bernardino County...are none too happy" about the Kaiser "invasion" of their region, voicing strong opposition to the favoritism shown to Kaiser Company. Local politicians elected to throw their support behind the new industrial venture, however, which presented a dynamic and lucrative future, even if local farmers, who represented the area's past, did not like it.

Kaiser Makes Peace with Labor

Keeping workers on the job and producing efficiently was critical, so Henry Kaiser had to change the way he dealt with labor. Kaiser Company was making an important transition in the late 1930s and early 1940s, from a construction outfit that largely hired workers as needed from local labor pools for individual jobs to a manufacturing concern, fixed in place, that needed a permanent supply of workers.

Kaiser did not have to worry about labor issues nearly as much while a construction man. At about the same time that Kaiser led his company into manufacturing, he also developed a more liberal, nonconfrontational, cooperative labor policy. For the first twenty years of his career as a businessman, though, Henry Kaiser held views toward unions that were commonly held among managers and owners nationwide: he hated them. According to Kaiser Company insider Gerard Piel, the Boss "was first a non-union man, but when he started working for Uncle Sam, he had to negotiate with unions. This turned around his labor polices 180 degrees." More to the point, when Kaiser began accepting contracts from the labor-friendly administration of President Franklin Roosevelt, he came to accept the idea of collective bargaining and that he had better deal with unions amicably rather than fight them at every corner. Having tied himself to Washington's purse strings for obtaining projects, acquiring approval and securing funding, beginning with projects engaged in after 1933, Henry Kaiser recognized the benefits of following New Deal labor edicts. Kaiser himself pointed out this transformation in a 1942 address to the National Press Club, admitting, "I didn't believe in unions at all many years ago; I wouldn't hire union men for the job. When the Government decided that men should be organized and that we should have collective bargaining I decided that I should abide by what the Government wanted to do, whether I agreed with it or not." He seems to have been driven by pragmatism. If labor had the right to organize, then management and workers could reach conciliation, and maybe the company could even reap gains in productivity. Kaiser became a zealot, an apostle, of the cause in the years ahead. Labor relations changed dramatically at Kaiser Company in the mid-1930s. The Hoover Dam project began during Herbert Hoover's term as president, and at that point, Kaiser still harbored a clear anti-union labor policy. Shortly after construction began in 1931, complaints by workers began to surface. Unskilled workers laboring in the canyon claimed that room and board costs consumed almost half their pay. Heat prostration alone killed fourteen workers between June 25 and July 16, 1931. One group of workers sued the consortium building the dam because of carbon monoxide poisoning men who were laboring in tunnels at the site. The consortium settled out of court with the workers and paid them a hefty $4.8 million award. Biographer Mark Foster concluded that "Kaiser later earned a well-deserved reputation as an enlightened entrepreneur in labor relations, but these qualities were not evident at least publicly in the early 1930s."

Burned at Hoover Dam by stinging publicity and costly litigation, Kaiser abruptly switched gears in his approach to unions. In 1937, he actually facilitated the organization efforts of the American Federation of Labor (AFL) at his Northern California aggregate plant. Since these workers were permanent, not to be released after the job ended, Kaiser's actions represented a new commitment on his part to collective bargaining over the long term. At the company's next construction job, the colossal Grand Coulee Dam on the Columbia River, Kaiser management again worked with, rather than against, unions. At Grand Coulee, Kaiser signed contracts with labor unions to represent workers without putting up a fight and went a step further, or perhaps a leap further, by offering workers the revolutionary Kaiser Health Plan, the precursor of what would become Kaiser Permanente, the nation's largest health maintenance organization. The Kaiser Health Plan quickly made its way to other elements of the ever-growing Kaiser industrial empire. Other titans of industry resisted cooperating with labor, like Henry Ford and the leaders of smaller steel firms, who refused to abide by some or all of the new labor laws, resulting in violent protest and bloodshed. Henry Kaiser had some mighty small shoes to fill as a steel company president, in the eyes of American labor. Kaiser's journey to become "labor's best friend," a moniker he wore with great pride, had begun.

Both the Metal Trades Union, affiliated with the AFL, and United Steelworkers of America (USWA), affiliated with the Congress of Industrial Organizations (CIO), campaigned vigorously to represent production workers at Fontana, with management not impeding their efforts. Kaiser's steelworkers handed the USWA-CIO a 2–1 vote of approval. With the results of this election, henceforth Fontana's production and maintenance workers would be members of United Steelworkers of America, Local 2869. The company could have held out for a wage scale a few cents an hour lower or offered less ample benefits. Instead, they earned the loyalty of CIO rank and file, leadership and even some radical elements within the union by taking a more conciliatory approach in this first labor contact. The CIO's California newspaper, the *Labor Herald*, a left-leaning press organ that regularly savaged all industrialists and business leaders (including Henry J. previously!) on principle, nonetheless called the labor agreement with Kaiser Company "one of the best in the nation." The union had been pressing for a seventeen-cent-an-hour raise at steel plants nationwide, but the industry resisted. Kaiser, on the other hand, just ceded the position. The CIO convinced Kaiser to agree to institute popular wage "incentive" plans at several of the mills at the Fontana plant; these plans paid workers in a handful of jobs more for production in excess of a certain base amount. Kaiser's popular health plan was first seen at the Grand Coulee project. The plan provided complete hospitalization in a fully equipped facility on the Fontana plant grounds and covered workers' lab work, surgery, nursing services and other care; the facility grew and later moved off site. Each participating employee paid just sixty cents per week, another sixty cents for each additional adult covered, and then thirty cents for each dependent child covered, all of which was payroll deductible (this later expanded off the plant site to also cover non-Kaiser workers). In a rare expression of praise for a capitalist, the CIO's *Labor Herald* boldly predicted that "in more ways than one the Henry J. Kaiser–United Steelworkers of America contract at Fontana sets a pattern that should ease transition from present to a future of full employment." If there was any residual tension between the labor and "the old Henry Kaiser," it could not be found. To underscore that this idea of Kaiser being "labor's best friend" was not just the product of a company PR campaign or the personal connection between one labor leader and one businessman, in 1990, the U.S. Department of Labor added Kaiser to the Labor Hall of Honor.

Interestingly, Henry Kaiser chose not to challenge widely accepted rules limiting the role of women in steel production jobs at the new Fontana plant. Even during the extreme labor shortages precipitated by World War II, American steel companies hired a surprisingly small number of women for production jobs—usually visually inspecting tin plate or as common laborers—seldom exceeding 10 percent of their total workforce. On the other hand, employers, including Kaiser Company, hired women by the tens of thousands to make ships; women might make up one-third of all workers at a shipyard. The steel industry proved to be much more resistant to breaking down barriers for women than most, even in the case of Kaiser, who had trailblazed with women shipbuilding.

Within a few years of launching the Fontana plant, Henry Kaiser began to receive widespread recognition for the strife-free labor relations at his operations. Approving observers characterized Henry Kaiser as an

Almost no women held production jobs at the Fontana plant until the tin mill opened, but a few women held jobs in the on-site chemical lab.

Now that the Gals are in the Field

Today—   Soon—

To address the uneasiness some men felt about working with women at the Fontana plant, the *Snorter* ran cartoons like this in 1943.

innovative, liberal, progressive or enlightened employer. He even won awards for his practices of accepting the right of his workers to organize, signing contracts without inducing work stoppages and offering benefits like the health plan. For example, in April 1944, La Salle College in Philadelphia honored the western industrialist for rendering "the most conspicuous and constructive service to the cause of industrial peace in America." In his address, Kaiser pointed to commonalities between labor and management, notably their shared responsibility for achieving the labor harmony at Kaiser enterprises. "Fundamentally the interests of labor and management are one," Kaiser opined. Men on the two sides are "members of the same family...the enterprise family." Spinning the complexities of labor relations into his own simpler branch of folksy wisdom, Kaiser said, in a line repeated innumerable times in the years ahead, that "labor relations [are] nothing more than human relations....There is neither secret nor mystery to labor relations. There is no need for a complicated formula, or for cumbersome

Henry Kaiser rarely visited his far-flung production sites, but he did visit this West Coast Kaiser shipyard in 1944 with his wife, Bess.

legislation." The United Steelworkers of America actually invited Kaiser to their national convention in May 1944 as their keynote speaker. Phil Murray introduced Kaiser to the 2,400 delegates by stating that "his outlook in the field of labor relations, as far as industry goes, has not been excelled by any industrialist in this country," which had earned him "the respect and admiration of the United Steelworkers of America, and particularly its president." After Kaiser sat down, Murray then took his turn to speak, moving his remarks in a more emotional direction, saying, "I wish that our nation had more Henry Kaisers," and unexpectedly adding, "We like you." Just a few years after embracing collective bargaining, Kaiser's actions and words had won him wide admiration. Some even pointed to the industrialist/labor leader as a potential running mate for FDR in the 1944 election. The remarkable speed with which Fontana began production owed a great debt to a developing Kaiser labor policy that had many of its kinks worked out at other projects. Fontana would see this progressive labor policy born to its full fruition.

THE FINAL TALLY

Kaiser Company's Fontana steelworks amassed an impressive wartime production record and prepared the Kaiser assault on the peacetime steel market. The upstart operation produced about 1.2 million tons of steel during the war, enough of the metal to build about two hundred cargo ships. Of the 1,209,000 tons of steel Kaiser Company's plant produced, 547,000 tons were ship plate (some 45.2 percent of total steel produced), 135,000 tons were steel shapes, 94,000 tons were shell steel (enough for about a million artillery shells) and 17,000 tons were bars (which could be rolled into any number of shapes). Kaiser silenced many of his critics with Fontana's breathtaking start-up and production performance; many had believed Kaiser would fail. No less than the industry's leading publication, *Iron Age*, predicted that Fontana reaching its seemingly impossible production goals in 1943 would be "nothing short of miraculous." But Fontana's record proved the naysayers wrong. A grateful federal government recognized the plant, its workers and its managers in several ways. On May 27, 1944, the U.S. Maritime Commission bestowed on Kaiser Company, Iron and Steel Division its Maritime (or M) Award for outstanding production achievement, giving each Kaiser employee a commemorative button. Kaiser's plant certainly compared favorably to the war record of its newest western integrated competitor, the Geneva,

PRESENTATION PROGRAM

MARITIME AWARD FOR
PRODUCTION ACHIEVEMENT

KAISER STEEL

Program cover for the ceremony marking Kaiser Steel receiving the Maritime Award from the navy, 1944.

Utah, plant built by the Defense Plant Corporation (DPC) and operated by U.S. Steel. Geneva received approval to be built about half a year before Fontana, but Fontana started producing steel in 1943, about one year before the Utah-based plant. The DPC built the Geneva plant using nearly twice the money Fontana cost (approximately $100 million for Fontana vs. $200

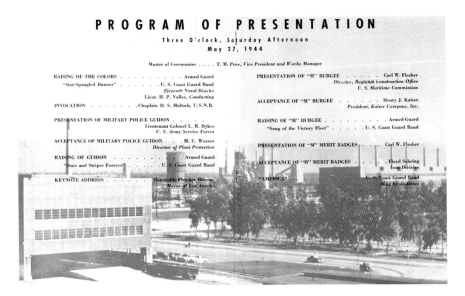

The list of events at the 1944 Maritime Award ceremony.

million for Geneva), and while the Utah plant had roughly twice the rated capacity of Fontana, Kaiser's facility outproduced its competitor during the war by a small margin (1.2 million tons for Fontana vs. 1.145 million tons for Geneva). Kaiser proved that he could make steel in Fontana, although the profitability of the plant remained in question. With one eye on the war and the other on the future, Henry Kaiser was already positioning the Fontana steelworks, which Kaiser employee Tom Price affectionately referred to as the Fontana "love child," for an assault on the peacetime steel market before World War II had even ended.

CHAPTER 3

KAISER STEEL AND THE WEST GROW, 1945–58

CONVERSION FROM WARTIME AND EXPANSION OF OPERATIONS

When World War II ended in 1945, the region had been transformed. The federal government spent about $40 billion on bases, factories and other projects in the American West during the war years. Before the war, coastal shipyards built virtually no cargo vessels at all, but new shipyards built by the government allowed the Pacific Coast to fabricate about one-half of the cargo ships built in America during the war. Aluminum, steel and magnesium plants sprang up across the West. Steelmaking capacity in the West roughly doubled in the war years, from 2.2 to 4.9 million tons. The wartime federal spending transformed Los Angeles from the nation's seventh-largest manufacturing center in 1939 to the second largest in 1944, but cities in the Rocky Mountain, Southwest, and Pacific Northwest states all benefited. In total, about eight million persons moved west in the 1940s. Clearly, the nation, especially the West, the area the Fontana steel plant set out to serve, emerged from World War II vastly different from when it had entered it.

With vivid memories of the long and grueling Great Depression still fresh in everyone's minds, labor activists, government officials and business leaders all speculated on whether or not wartime spending had fixed the disastrous economic problems of the 1930s. Referring to his state's outlook for the future, California governor Earl Warren, an optimist, said in 1945,

The recent westward flow of people—that is, steel consumers—is noted in this postwar Kaiser Steel brochure.

"We have sniffed our destiny." Similarly, A.P. Giannini of Bank of America looked to the region's bright future when he said, "The West Coast hasn't even started yet." In 1945, Henry Kaiser and United Auto Workers (UAW) president R.J. Thomas met to discuss ways for organized labor and industry to cooperate and create a national economy supporting sixty million jobs. During their meeting, they paid particular attention to new industrial jobs in the West, with Thomas saying, "The kind of initiative I have seen here at the Kaiser enterprises encourages me to believe that we can solve the problem [of creating jobs] on the West Coast and over the entire nation. The resources are waiting, labor is ready, and large sections of management indicate their desire to cooperate." West Coast director of the UAW Cy O'Halloran revealed in August 1945 that he would be "tickled to death" if the new Michigan-based Kaiser-Frazer automobile venture opened an assembly plant in California and promised, "We'll help Kaiser with everything in our power to see to it that parts are made available to him." Kaiser-Frazer built very few cars on the West Coast in two short-lived plants, but that did not dissuade Henry Kaiser from making eyebrow-raising proposals, like one in 1946 to build two million low-cost homes, which received hearty labor approval. By the end of the war, Kaiser's success at bringing thousands of new high-paying union jobs to the West Coast made labor leaders believers in Henry Kaiser.

Even with all the talk of cooperation with Big Labor, Kaiser's steel plant could not lead the West into a new industrial era with the limited steelmaking capacity and small product line it had in 1945. There was no longer much need for artillery shell casings or ship plate (Kaiser's last bit of shipbuilding ended in 1946), leaving the plant ill-suited for peacetime demand. The Fontana steelworks could make a small range of steel shapes, but it did not have the capability to make widely used civilian products such as pipe, sheet for appliance or auto manufacture, tin plate or zinc plate (galvanized) products. Wisely, Kaiser managers made a first small step in readying the plant for the peacetime economy by building a blooming mill in 1944. Blooming mills provided a primary, efficiency-adding step. Acting like a giant clothes wringer, a blooming mill passed red-hot ingots between massive rolls, making shapes called blooms and slabs. Before erecting its blooming mill, the Fontana plant had to pour smaller ingots, which necessitated making more pourings, a process that left Kaiser at a higher cost disadvantage compared to other producers. Fontana was further hampered by having a small steelmaking capacity at the war's end. Fontana's yearly steelmaking capacity in 1945 of seven hundred thousand ingot tons would make it a large plant by West Coast standards but too small to grow the western steel market as Kaiser wanted.

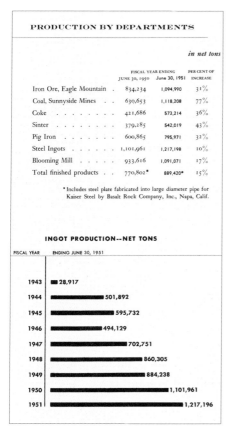

PRODUCTION BY DEPARTMENTS

in net tons

	FISCAL YEAR ENDING JUNE 30, 1950	June 30, 1951	PER CENT OF INCREASE
Iron Ore, Eagle Mountain	834,234	1,094,990	31%
Coal, Sunnyside Mines	630,653	1,118,208	77%
Coke	421,686	573,214	36%
Sinter	379,285	542,019	43%
Pig Iron	600,865	795,971	32%
Steel Ingots	1,101,961	1,217,198	10%
Blooming Mill	933,616	1,091,071	17%
Total finished products	770,802*	889,420*	15%

*Includes steel plate fabricated into large diameter pipe for Kaiser Steel by Basalt Rock Company, Inc., Napa, Calif.

INGOT PRODUCTION--NET TONS

FISCAL YEAR   ENDING JUNE 30, 1951

1943	28,917
1944	501,892
1945	595,732
1946	494,129
1947	702,751
1948	860,305
1949	884,238
1950	1,101,961
1951	1,217,196

Fontana's uneven steel production in its first few years is shown in this table.

Entering the postwar market, steel demand slumped badly, so Fontana's meager output in 1945 and 1946 depressed the plant's operating efficiency and, therefore, profitability. In fact, right after the war ended, the amount of steel leaving the plant gates was so low that Fontana stood the very real possibility of defaulting on its Reconstruction Finance Corporation loan repayments. In 1945, the Kaiser plant produced 595,732 ingot tons of steel; in 1946, that amount fell to 494,129 ingot tons, nearly a 20 percent drop. Kaiser Company still owed the RFC nearly $100 million at that point, and with the Fontana operation still operating in the red, the company needed relief fast.

In early February 1945, however, Henry Kaiser's conversion plans for Fontana received an unforeseen and unwanted challenge from U.S. Steel. Out of the blue, the president of U.S. Steel offered to purchase the Geneva works it was operating from the Defense Plant Corporation—and also purchase Kaiser's Fontana plant. Geneva faced a high price tag on its conversion to peacetime production, as well: some $50–$60 million, by one estimate. Of course, U.S. Steel had very deep pockets, with assets totaling over $2 billion. Needless to say, Kaiser felt threatened. "Fontana is not and will not be for sale," he shot back just days later. "The Kaiser Company is still at a loss to understand why the United States Steel Corporation writes the Defense Plant Corporation making an offer for the Kaiser Company's property." Blunting Fairless's jab, Henry Kaiser then counterpunched by announcing that "the Kaiser Company is making a study of Geneva with a view of determining whether Geneva would be a contribution or a compliment [*sic*] to the Fontana mill, or to the West, and if so it will likewise, request the same opportunity to make a proposal to the Government for the purchase or lease exactly as the United States Steel Corporation has announced it will do." For whatever reason (and Kaiser's volatile and raw relationship with Fairless might have been reason enough), in the press, Kaiser continued to explore options to acquire the Geneva plant. It seemed exactly what one magazine called in 1945 "The Battle of the Giants."

Then in July 1945, as the war in the Pacific approached its sudden and fiery conclusion, Kaiser surprised everyone when he announced his interest in creating an "independent Western steel syndicate" of steelmakers. This syndicate would include the new integrated plants at Geneva and Fontana, the established Colorado integrated producer in Pueblo, CF & I, and a number of smaller "melt shops," a group of producers collectively worth some $350 million. The federal government might have helped Kaiser enter steelmaking in 1942, but by the early postwar period, it had pulled back from that additional support. Henry Kaiser met with CF & I's top manager,

Charles Allen—who had expressed interest in buying the Geneva plant, too, in early July 1945—to discuss the possibility of some kind of collective strategy to challenge U.S. Steel. Just days after this tête-à-tête, *Business Week* interviewed Allen because of the fury that the Kaiser/CF & I talks had created. Allen knocked down the rumors of a merger, saying, "It has us married when we're not even engaged." Kaiser kept right on talking anyway. As to who would fund the steel combination, in his statements, Henry Kaiser casually dropped the name of Bank of America, the nation's second-largest financial institution and a longtime supporter of various Kaiser enterprises. He seemed to relish the fight.

During this media war, the Reconstruction Finance Corporation offered Kaiser Company some relief on its Fontana loan. In late July 1945, the RFC announced that it could offer more money to Kaiser Company explicitly for conversion purposes: $114.3 million. In addition, the RFC debt could be broken up into three parts: a $69.5 million fifteen-year first mortgage at 4 percent interest, a second $34.5 million twenty-five-year mortgage without interest and a $10.4 million note secured by Kaiser Company stock. This was not the deal he wanted, but Henry Kaiser accepted nonetheless. These conditions (and other less significant ones) gave Kaiser Company a bit of breathing room at a crucial time. However, the deal did not substantially alter Fontana's long-term indebtedness, and because it forced Kaiser Company to turn over 25 percent of its Iron and Steel Division profits toward payment of the second mortgage, it severely hindered the company's ability to fund a major expansion in the future. If anything, the meager kindness to Kaiser from RFC only redoubled Henry's efforts to seek other means to pay off the RFC as soon as possible. Kaiser management was at a loss for how to explain the dramatic change in posture from Washington toward their company and their boss. Perhaps the election-year probe of the RFC and other federal agencies by Congress, looking for waste and fraud and to discredit long-term Democratic leadership in Washington, poisoned the waters for Kaiser Steel. Years later, Al Heiner wrote, "In retrospect, it is hard to comprehend why Kaiser could not get the RFC to grant him even the tiniest adjustment on his steel loans. Here was Kaiser, the best-known and possibly best-liked industrialist to come upon the high level Washington, D.C. scene."

Kaiser did not have to look hard to find plenty of supporters in his efforts to soften up the RFC. The Congress of Industrial Organizations considered the RFC's tough stance with Fontana on financing to be a "body blow to the West's hopes for a steel industry." With the prospect of many thousands of industrial jobs hanging in the balance of maintaining the West's new steel plants, the union dedicated itself to Kaiser's cause. In fact, the union stated that one of its "main peacetime tasks" was to "enlist in the current struggle to an expanded western steel industry." In 1946, California's popular governor Earl Warren wrote a letter to Congress asking for a favorable renegotiation of Kaiser's RFC loan because "of all the war-induced development on industry in our State no unit is of greater importance than the Fontana Steel Mill, constructed for war needs it can become a foundation for great industrial advances in peacetime." Clearly, Kaiser's steelworks, along with that of U.S. Steel in Geneva, had excited many labor leaders, regional boosters and political figures. Of course, Kaiser did have detractors. For example, a mid-1940s editorial in the *Chicago Tribune* blasted Kaiser's Washington connections, arguing that "Henry J. Kaiser's exploits have won him nationwide attention. He built gigantic dams on Government money, cargo vessels on Government money, and made magnesium and steel on Government money. Now he's taking off on other ventures, with Government blessing, if not money." Another editorial in the *Tribune* five months later echoed this harsh criticism: "It is very easy to be a liberal in the Kaiser sense when it pays such handsome returns....Kaiser is not an industrialist in the ordinary sense that an industrialist is an entrepreneur whose talents attract risk capital for the support of his ventures....The Government has subsidized him and passed along the risks to taxpayers who foot the bill without even having a voice in the matter."

In 1946, it appeared that some Washington agencies were retreating from their initial demand to exact top dollar for the West's steel plants. After initially expressing interest in buying Geneva, then feigning trepidation, U.S. Steel finally offered the DPC $40 million for the plant, about one fifth of what it cost to build. The government accepted the low offer, and even Kaiser initially hailed the transaction as a boon to the West.

Yet in spite of all Kaiser's efforts, plus the efforts of his influential supporters, the RFC did not cut any of Kaiser's debt on the Fontana facility; the $114.3 million package was all Kaiser received. None of the books written on Henry Kaiser have been able to explain why the RFC dealt with Kaiser so strictly and the DPC dealt with U.S. Steel so favorably, and records on this decision are sketchy, but Kaiser looked at it as an outrage and completely unacceptable, government favoritism of the most pernicious and destructive type, picking one private sector concern over another arbitrarily. Rebuffed by the Reconstruction Finance Corporation, Kaiser had to find another means to pay off this debt. A furious Kaiser issued numerous press releases and brochures—one of which, since

Kaiser took the government policies personally, was titled "Outrage in Steel, as told by Henry J. Kaiser." In it, he accused the government of "undermining competition and fostering monopoly…menacing a basic industry needed by the entire nation…[and] threatening failure of hundreds of manufacturers," among other things. It is unclear how widely read or discussed this brochure was, but since the RFC did not change its position, the brochure can't be judged as being terribly effective.

During this period, Fontana planners moved ahead with some retooling and expansion of the product line. To that end, in 1945, Kaiser Company opened a merchant mill at Fontana, financed through private sources. The mill housed machines that rolled steel into round, flat and square bars, as well as some small structural shapes. Kaiser managers further improved the company's ability to serve the postwar industrial economy by adding a skelp mill in 1947. This mill produced the material from which pipe, called skelp, was made. Adding a skelp mill promised to pay big dividends for the company, allowing it better take advantage of both the house-building boom predicted to hit California and the nationwide gas pipe–laying boom that was already underway. Kaiser Company followed up on this by opening a continuous-weld pipe mill in January 1948. This mill produced pipe from one-half to four inches in diameter that found use in household plumbing. Proving the decision to enter the pipe business a wise move, a large-diameter pipe deal was Kaiser's first really big steel contract signed after the war. According to Al Heiner, this one deal "was the most important in Kaiser Steel's history because in large measure it funded the transition from wartime to peacetime manufacturing facilities.…[Fontana was] saved by the market." Kaiser signed a deal with the Transcontinental Gas Pipe Line Company in September 1948 for 470,000 tons of steel in the form of thirty-inch-diameter pipe, requiring some twenty thousand railcars to carry, that Transcontinental planned to lay from Texas to New York. These numbers sound huge; indeed, the *Ingot* reported that this project would create the longest natural gas pipeline in the world. Although the deal was outside the western service area Kaiser normally attracted, Transcontinental could not find another producer capable of delivering on time. Since Kaiser's rolling facilities could not yet accommodate this order, Fontana made the steel, rolled it into sheet, then sent the sheet to another steel company for rolling into pipe. Kaiser could produce the steel in a timely manner, and the Los Angeles–based Western Manufacturers could roll it into pipe. Sensing a customer with the means to pay (a notable Henry Kaiser skill), Kaiser Steel passed along some of the expansion costs to Transcontinental, which paid a hefty thirty dollars more per ton than the going market rate, and this emboldened Kaiser management to mark up prices across its product line. Kaiser Steel was now running the Fontana plant at full capacity, and the company charged customers a premium price for its product, resulting in the Fontana operation posting its first profits from steelmaking in 1948, an outcome that continued for the next few years.

In addition to offering a greater variety of steel products, in the early postwar period, Kaiser Steel increased its capacity to make steel. Fontana's yearly steel production, boosted by the pipe sale, jumped over 30 percent, from 494,129 tons in 1946 to 860,305 tons in 1948, and began to run up against its iron making capacity. So, in 1948 and 1949, Fontana added a second blast furnace, its seventh open hearth furnace and an additional forty-five coke ovens to boost capacity.

Kaiser Steel moved on the supply side as well. In 1946, Kaiser Company concluded negotiations begun during the war with Southern Pacific Railroad (SP) to purchase the undeveloped Eagle Mountain iron mine in Riverside County. This deal meant that Kaiser Steel could retire Vulcan Mine, which was ending its productive life anyway. The company made the improvements needed to transform Eagle Mountain into a modern, cost-efficient mine,

Eagle Mountain mine had more and more elaborate worker housing than Vulcan; a preliminary ore processing facility is in the background, circa 1960.

and it became Fontana's chief source of ore for the rest of its history. In August 1948, Eagle Mountain iron ore began to be dug and prepared for use at the Fontana plant; the first actual shipment took place two months later. The giant mine promised to be worth every bit of the wait and legal hassle. Geologists speculated that Eagle Mountain contained tens of millions of tons of ore, enough for decades of steelmaking at Fontana. There was so much ore there, in fact, that by the early 1960s, Kaiser was exporting some ore to Japan. At slightly over 50 percent iron content, the ore was of good quality. With much of the overburden removed, miners could then extract the ore by the economical open pit method. Miners loosened the ore with explosive charges, then huge power shovels and draglines scooped up the ore and dumped it into massive trucks, which drove a short distance to waiting railcars. Crews built a fifty-two-mile spur from the mine to SP rails at Ferrum (*ferrum* is the Latin word for iron) near the Salton Sea. Kaiser Steel owned the fifty-two miles of track and the railcars and locomotives that operated on it. At Ferrum, SP trains took the ore and pulled it to Fontana. To drive down transportation costs, Kaiser Steel operated "unitized" railcars on its short line: a uniform number of railcars and locomotives, each car loaded with a predetermined amount of ore (approximately sixty tons per car at first), mated with a specific number of locomotives of a given horsepower. Within a few years, KSC added facilities at Eagle Mountain to minimally process the ore by pelletizing, making every load of ore more concentrated in iron content to enhance efficiency. In 1958, Southern Pacific bumped up the mine's productivity another notch by replacing its sixty-ton railcars with ones of one-hundred-ton capacity. Kaiser's 164-mile haul for iron was a reasonable length by industry standards. KSC addressed the needs of mine workers in those years, too. Mine workers and their families—soon numbering over five hundred, with more to follow in coming years—lived on-site in a company town. To the original two dozen homes hastily constructed to begin operations, Kaiser Company added more and improved homes and supporting services. Just as Fontana looked like no other steel plant, Eagle Mountain looked like no other mining town. Lawns and trees surrounded the homes, and the isolated company town boasted of having a theater, swimming pool, playgrounds and other facilities; the lunar-like surrounding mountains made for a dramatic backdrop. The company made Los Angeles–based television channels available to residents. Eagle Mountain was hardly a resort, but it was an oasis of sorts in the rugged desert. The acquisition of Eagle Mountain, a good mine at a reasonable distance from the plant, secured Kaiser Company's place as an integrated steel producer.

ORE TRAIN LEAVING EAGLE MOUNTAIN MINE

Kaiser Steel began using unit trains early in Eagle Mountain's life to control ore costs.

Blast furnace no. 3 under construction in 1953.

If Kaiser Steel was to become a permanent fixture in Southern California, having to exist alongside the region's ever-growing population, its managers would have to remain mindful of the plant's pollution, especially that of the air. Addressing the issue of airborne emissions, in 1949, the company established its Fume Investigation Department, which consisted of four people who monitored emissions and developed means to control it. The year 1952 brought a name change to reflect the company's aggressive commitment to air pollution: the Air Quality Control and Research Department. By 1954, that department had grown to fifteen technicians, engineers and chemists engaged in pollution recording and research. Some tangible fruits of these commitments came in 1954, when the company began installing electrostatic precipitators on the stacks of Fontana's nine open hearth furnaces to trap particle matter in gas, visible to the eye as smoke. The equipment, which cost the firm several million dollars, trapped about 95 percent of the solids from leaving the stacks, making the exhaust dramatically less dark and offensive. But the technology available at the time did not trap poisonous gases, so tackling the most challenging air pollution offenders, the hundreds of coke ovens, would have to wait. In the meantime, KSC would feel increased pressure to clean up its various emissions from a growing number of regulatory agencies. Beginning in the late 1940s, the Los Angeles Air Pollution Control District exerted ever more demands on KSC to invest ever greater amounts of money into air pollution abatement; state and then federal regulation came later. The growing steel plant, with its many stacks and exhaust that could be easily seen and smelled, was an easy target, even as millions of cars drove in the area, every one of them burning gasoline yet (at that point) lacking a single emission control device. Even the industry-friendly County of San Bernardino government began to clamp down on air polluters in 1956 with the creation of the San Bernardino County Air Pollution District. Southern California agencies wrote the world's strictest air pollution standards.

After failing to get the RFC to budge on its position concerning Kaiser's debt for Fontana, in 1950, Kaiser Steel finally secured private funding to pay off its government debt and then to fund some much-needed expansion. Bank of America's Amadeo Giannini introduced Henry Kaiser to George Woods of the First Boston Company, who assembled the private sector financing package. Kaiser Steel's fortunes had improved in 1948 and 1949; plus, it had been given a clean bill of health by a widely known consulting firm in 1949, so Woods felt KSC was a good risk. The package consisted of $25 million in loans from several banks (including Kaiser friend and project underwriter Giannini), $60 million in mortgage bonds purchased from ten major insurance companies and $40 million raised from the sale of 1.6 million stock "units" (each unit consisted of one share of preferred stock and one-half share of common stock). The deal raised $125 million, enough to repay Kaiser's debt to the government and have some change leftover. In November 1950, a beaming Henry Kaiser presented a check to the Reconstruction Finance Corporation for $91,476,989.92. The check retired his debt and paid the government $1.23 for every dollar borrowed. Kaiser Company, Iron and Steel Division changed its name to Kaiser Steel Corporation (KSC) in 1950, maintaining its headquarters in Oakland, Kaiser Company's home base.

The $125 million infusion gave the Fontana plant at least a fighting chance at success in the steel business. Management kept moving aggressively on the raw materials front in April 1950 by purchasing Utah Fuel Company, operator of the Sunnyside coal mine. This single purchase satisfied most of Fontana's coal needs and allowed KSC to sell coal. The high costs for transporting one million tons of coal to Fontana every year by rail over extremely long distances, costs that analysts in the 1940s all recognized made Fontana a high-cost producer, were not alleviated by acquiring the Sunnyside mine—or Raton in New Mexico, purchased several years after Sunnyside. An 1,100-mile boat ride for coal by deep water would have been affordable, but Fontana's landlocked location precluded that attractive option. High coal costs continued to bedevil the company's Oakland "bean counters."

This financing package allowed Kaiser management to augment production, so an eighth blast furnace and a new mill were added. KSC leadership made an undeniably smart business move by opening a tin plate mill in 1951 at the Fontana plant. As stated in KSC's annual report from 1951, its first year to publish such a document as a publicly owned company, producing tin plate for cans enabled "a mill whose primary market is in a particular region to serve the needs of that region more completely." Indeed, for many years, tin plate manufacturing was the largest or nearly largest use of steel in the West. In the late 1940s and early 1950s, the West consumed about seven hundred thousand tons of tin plate yearly, about one-fourth of the nation's demand for cans, but until that time, nearly all of it came from the Midwest or the East. Arch-competitor U.S. Steel, through its subsidiary Columbia Steel, enlarged a tin-plating operation in Pittsburg, California (there's no *h* in this Pittsburg near Oakland) with a $25 million infusion in 1948; this facility used Geneva-made steel to make cans. This surely must

Washington Post

$123,305,000 Debt Repaid In Full by Kaiser Steel

WITH INTEREST—Henry J. Kaiser (left) is congratulated by RFC Vice Chairman C. Edward Rowe after the West Coast industrialist handed over a check for $91,476,958.92 as the last payment of a $123,305,000 loan on the Kaiser Steel Corp. plant at Fontana, Calif. About 23 million dollars in interest was included

Right: A thrilled HJK handing a huge check to a government official, paying off early the government loan for Fontana's expansion.

Below: The elaborate cover of the program for the big-budget celebration marking Kaiser Steel opening its tin plate mill in 1953.

THE INGOT

Vol. IV   DECEMBER 1, 1952   No. 23

ASSORTING TIN PLATE

A must demand of canning industry and tin plate trade is a luster finish on tin plate. The product is line inspected, with final inspection made by the metallurgical department. Shown in picture is Irene Talbott, assorter in the Electrolytic Dept.

An image of a tin mill assorter, or flipper, from the early 1950s.

have spurred Henry J. He ordered his new mill built with a two-hundred-thousand-ton annual capacity, the same as Pittsburg (although Kaiser Steel never made complete cans). Kaiser Steel spent $25 million on the nine-acre tin plate mill, which began limited production in August 1952. Although self-promotion was a Henry Kaiser trait, he really "pulled out all the stops" to mark this opening. The firm commandeered Conrad Hilton's Arrowhead Lodge in the San Gabriel Mountains overlooking the Los Angeles basin for several days in December 1951. The event was immortalized on a brilliant multicolored brochure. Guests dined on green turtle au sherry soup and lemon sole sauté amadine, sipped California wine and enjoyed the serenading of up-and-coming pianist Liberace.

The new tin plate mill offered a new and regionally important product line for the company, and it provided the first production jobs of any significant number for women at the Fontana plant. Until this mill opened, women were, for all practical purposes, excluded from any other production jobs at the plant. And following accepted steel industry practice, KSC management hired women exclusively for a select few critical jobs in the new mill. The primary jobs these women landed were as "assorters," workers who visually inspected tin-plated steel sheets for flaws. Steel mill managers across America and across many decades generally believed women to be superior to men at inspecting tin plate. These male managers believed that women not only had a keener eye for detail but also could better deal with the tedium of the job. Mildred Foust was a top-ranking woman in Kaiser's tin mill and remembered that Kaiser officials did briefly consider using men in the new facility. She recalled, "They weren't quite sure when they were first talking about it whether or not they would hire men from the service, disabled veterans," but after briefly experimenting with men as assorters, they found that "it was too tedious a work [and men] couldn't sit on the machines as long." Although these women carried United Steelworkers of America cards, they could only fill a narrow range of jobs, with no options for advancement (lines of progression). In the 1950s, Kaiser Steel employed, at any one time, over two hundred women as assorters or, as they often called themselves, "flippers" or "tin mill girls." Former flipper Gussie Heaton recalled how those "sheets of tin were thin, like very thin. And when you turn one over, if you turn them just right when you hit the fore corner, the corner pops right up. So you had to learn that when you get it up in the air, you give it a little lift, and that corner will hit first and you won't damage it. Took me about two months to learn that!" The best flippers working at maximum speed, such as in a competition, could inspect one-and-one-half tons of tin in thirty minutes. Tin flippers often landed their jobs right off the street as a job class five, which paid $2.01 per hour in 1956, the same as some office workers.

The 1950 refinancing gave Kaiser Steel the expansion of operations and materials that it needed to be competitive in a fast-moving and cutthroat

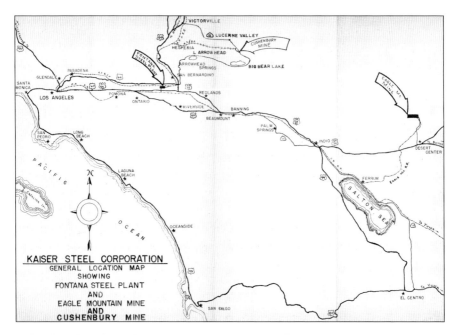

Kaiser Steel firmed up mineral sourcing in the 1950s; KSC's coal assets, being about one thousand miles from the plant, were far beyond this map.

industry, but expansion at Fontana in the postwar period continued—it had to. In the mid-1950s, Kaiser Steel further strengthened its raw materials holdings with two more important purchases. In 1955, KSC bought a limestone quarry seventy-five miles north of Fontana, in the Lucerne Valley. Until making this purchase, KSC obtained this essential blast furnace fluxing ingredient off the market from Nevada and elsewhere. The Cushenbury site interested Kaiser management because of its proximity to Fontana and because of limestone's shared importance in cement making. Kaiser's Permanente Cement Company, which shared top leadership and a parent company headquartered in Oakland with KSC, split the quarry development costs as well as its output. Santa Fe Railroad constructed a thirty-mile rail spur from the mine to an existing rail line to transport the limestone. Kaiser secured control of even more coking coal that same year, but unfortunately, it was nowhere near as close as Cushenbury. KSC acquired the real estate and mining rights of the St. Louis, Rocky Mountain and Pacific Company near Raton, New Mexico, 1,100 miles from Fontana. The transaction gave KSC title to over 202,950 acres of coal-bearing land and mining rights to another 326,854 acres, making this the largest area of coal land ownership in America at the time. The Raton mine could satisfy Fontana's yearly coal appetite for hundreds of years of steelmaking. The coal mined at Raton could also be sold to customers in a variety of industries, such as to utilities companies, which wanted coal with low sulfur content, providing KSC steady income.

In the mid-1950s, the young and aggressive management team started to enhance KSC's vertical integration by acquiring regional steel-using businesses. Launching this trend, KSC purchased Myers Drum Company in Los Angeles in March 1954, giving Kaiser control of an established producer of steel drums (primarily thirty- and fifty-gallon) and pails that served the western paint, chemical and petroleum industries. Myers fabricated four thousand steel drums and ten thousand steel pails every day. In 1955, KSC purchased the California-based Basalt Rock Company, firming up its presence in the booming western pipe market. Basalt Rock was the West's largest producer of large-diameter pipe, employing about 750 people. The superheated postwar western construction industry gobbled up pipe of all diameters and applications. Basalt Rock had two sites: one in Fontana and another in Napa on the north end of San Francisco Bay. Basalt Rock fabricated steel structures on-site or on location, including tanks, towers, highway overpasses and buildings. Complementing the Basalt Rock purchase was the 1955 purchase of Union Steel Company of Montebello in east Los Angeles. These two firms comprised the new fabricating division of Kaiser Steel Corporation, added one thousand people to the KSC payroll

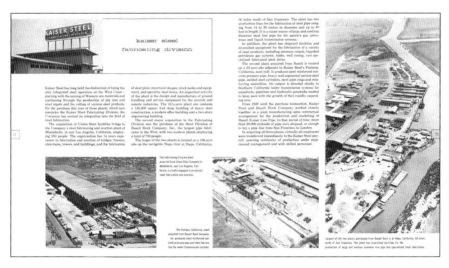

With the purchase of fabrication companies, Kaiser Steel production expanded from Fontana into Los Angeles, the San Francisco Bay Area and beyond.

and ensured that steel poured and rolled at Fontana would find a buyer. The fabricating division of Kaiser Steel remained an essential part of the company, even outlasting steel production at Fontana by several years.

Clearly, the postwar moves made by KSC management benefited the western economy, from Fontana itself to areas many hundreds of miles away. In terms of specifics, by 1955, 319 western steel-consuming firms purchased Kaiser Steel pipe and about 550 purchased Kaiser Steel plate and sheet, which ended up as car bumpers, appliances, tanks, agricultural equipment and many other products. Through the 1950s, KSC sold over 75 percent of its steel in California, around 50 percent in Southern California alone. Steel-consuming companies in Los Angeles, such as General Motors, purchased steel poured and rolled in Fontana. Companies coming to Fontana in the plant's first ten years of operation that purchased steel from Kaiser included Basalt Rock, Graver Tank and Manufacturing, Taylor Forge and Pipe Works, Koppers Company, Dow Chemical and the Fontana Mineral Wool Company.

An important component in the West's postwar economic explosion came from new home construction, which created a voracious demand for steel, a demand Kaiser Steel focused on addressing. Kaiser Steel took advantage of California's ongoing population boom; about one thousand people moved to California each day in the mid-1950s. California overtook New York in the early 1960s as the nation's most populous state. To house these new residents, the state of California issued 254,000 building permits for new houses in 1954 alone, nearly one-fourth of the total in the entire nation that year. Kaiser could provide the pipe for natural gas pipelines and steel shapes for transmission towers.

Beginning in 1956, the Kaiser Steel Corporation launched another dramatic expansion program of its Fontana facilities. Kaiser Steel's general manager, Jack Ashby, announced Kaiser's program would boost steelmaking and rolling an impressive 40 percent and cost $113 million. Tin plate, steel plate, hot rolled sheet and structural sheet all got boosts through enlarged soaking pits, a new tin-plating line, a new slab mill (to roll ingots), a hot strip mill (to roll for the pipe mill, tin mill and other uses) and two new open hearth furnaces to produce more steel. Kaiser Steel's big surprise, though, came in embracing exciting, perhaps even revolutionary, new steelmaking technology in this expansion: state-of-the-art oxygen furnaces. Oxygen steelmaking came to America from Europe in the early 1950s, acquiring other names like the L-D process and the basic oxygen process, or BOP. Kaiser Steel became the first user of this technology in the American West.

Oxygen furnaces are more efficient in operation than open hearth furnaces, making steel in minutes rather than hours, oftentimes of higher quality. By the close of the twentieth century, oxygen dominated world steel production, and Kaiser Steel was a leader in its adoption.

Then just a few months after announcing this major expansion, before it had even finished the program, Kaiser Steel augmented the upgrade with an additional infusion of $81 million. The extra investment included building 90 coke ovens (bringing the total to 315, the number KSC would close with having), a fourth blast furnace (Fontana's last), a third oxygen furnace and improvements at Eagle Mountain, Raton, and Sunnyside. Financed by the sales of bonds and the use of cash on hand, the entire expansion doubled ingot capacity from 1.5 million tons per year to 2.9 million tons per year, created over two thousand new jobs and made Kaiser Steel the largest steel producer west of the Mississippi. Kaiser Steel was at least treading water, if not in fact swimming on its own, using private sector money to expand operations.

The more or less continuous expansion program of the company, coupled to the insatiable growth of KSC's service area, contributed to Kaiser Steel's steady profitability in the 1950s. After its first year as a publicly held company, 1951, KSC reported a modest profit of $7.5 million. Profit levels hovered around that level until 1956 and 1957, when they jumped to a more impressive $23.6 million and $21.4 million, respectively. But company management had hoped to be making those kinds of profits, or higher, for several years before 1956. The 1950s definitely ended on a sour note for Kaiser Steel's accountants, though, as it did for businesses across America. KSC profit

That is the story behind our No. 1 program. Kaiser Steel is going to be the No. 1 steel company in the nation!

fully on the economic goals of the company and then passed on to develop at length the many important goals in human relations, union relations, communications, safety, employee security and opportunities—all the things necessary for the company and employees to do to earn the right to be known as the NUMBER ONE steel company.

Opening Goals

Ashby referred to the fact that our company had been operating at higher rates than those of the national steel industry in the past several months. "You must know," he said "that we must operate at better than industry averages."

He explained this by saying that the company had borrowed heavily to finance mine and plant facilities which made it possible to increase employment and ex-

goals will be made known employees by their foremen a supervisors.

Employee Security

In speaking of Employee curity and Employee Opportity, Ashby said that these foll naturally when a company strong in sales, in production, earnings and profit—with pr leading to further expansions. pledged that Kaiser Steel wo continue to grow and maintain rightful position in the fast-gr ing West.

Union Relations

With regard to union relati Ashby paid tribute to the f cooperation between the co any and the union over the ye pointing out that our record marred by only one serious w stoppage.

He said that difficulties t (Continued on Page 7)

One of Kaiser Steel's mottos was "Together We Build," seen in this image from the *Ingot*, 1954.

levels in 1958 suffered during the sharp national recession, dropping to just $5.4 million. The following year brought no relief on the financial front; in fact, 1959 brought the company's first loss for the decade, $7.4 million, in part driven by the continuing recession but more a result of a long and bitter national steel strike, discussed later. While U.S. Steel and Bethlehem reported profits measured in hundreds of millions of dollars each year in the 1950s, the nation's ninth-largest steel firm could not even break $25 million. Entering the new decade of the 1960s, Kaiser Steel management looked to a profound change in the way it approached dealing with its workers as integral to how it would break out of its earnings doldrums.

"TOGETHER WE BUILD": LABOR RELATIONS 1945–58

The year 1959 should have been a banner year for the Kaiser Steel Corporation. The latest $200 million expansion had made Kaiser Steel the ninth-largest steel producer in the nation and, with the new three-furnace oxygen shop, among the most modern, too. Furthermore, Kaiser Steel Corporation realized profits every year from 1950 through 1958. How many industry observers would have predicted a record like this in 1942? But instead of being positive, 1959 turned out to be a horrible year for Kaiser Steel. Ironically, given Henry J. Kaiser's focus on maintaining peace on the labor front, a breakdown in labor relations in 1959 brought the first plant work stoppage authorized by the union in the company's seventeen-year history, dragging down the company's ledgers for the year deeply into the red. Both Kaiser and his lieutenants spent considerable time trying to make Kaiser Steel different from other steel companies in terms of the relationship between labor and management, but problems in that relationship existed nonetheless.

The lack of an authorized plant-wide strike at Kaiser Steel's Fontana works by its production and maintenance workers from 1942 until 1959 greatly facilitated the company's early success. Kaiser Steel kept production humming while its eastern competition regularly ground to a halt with almost every industry contract negotiation. Men in the Labor Relations Department at KSC were instructed by their superiors to "just get the job done"—that is, to settle grievances and sign contracts with a minimum of interruptions—and to avoid "downtime." Former Kaiser steelworker and USWA Local 2869 official John Piazza said, "I don't think that right after the war [Henry] Kaiser wanted a strike because Kaiser wanted to pay off

human
relations

The Key to Abundant Happiness

BY HENRY J. KAISER

Henry Kaiser's quotations and
speeches, often about labor relations,
were commonly distributed in press
releases, brochures and so forth.

debt and he was trying to expand the plant, so that's why labor relations were a little different at Kaiser." In fact, if KSC had followed the steel industry's pattern, Kaiser steelworkers would have walked off the job in 1946, 1949 and 1952, which were the years when binding industry-wide contracts lapsed before new ones could be signed. But KSC's steelworkers did not strike in those years.

Top-ranking labor leadership continued to have very amicable relations with Henry Kaiser and other leading company officials through the 1950s. After Phil Murray's death in 1952, his secretary of many years, David J. McDonald, replaced him as president of the United Steelworkers of America. McDonald seemed highly supportive of Kaiser and his labor policies, as can be gleaned from speeches the two men delivered at a conference in 1954. Both Kaiser and McDonald presented addresses at a seminar on human relations sponsored jointly by the University of California and the USWA at a retreat at Lake Arrowhead in the San Gabriel Mountains. The two men struck familiar tones in their remarks. Kaiser entitled his presentation, "Human Relations—The Key to Abundant Happiness." He invoked one of his favorite chestnuts: "Problems are only opportunity in work clothes." Successful labor relations sounded so easy when listening to Henry Kaiser. McDonald likewise struck conciliatory notes when speaking to 120 company and union leaders in Fontana the morning before the seminar. "The United Steelworkers of America are partners in the American Steel Industry," McDonald told his Fontana audience. The labor chief observed that because of federal labor legislation, "We are married, you know, now. There is no mother to go home to, and we can't get a divorce." McDonald underscored his clear rejection of the idea that unions created class conflict and stated, "We are all the same—Americans—there are no classes here." At the same time, while he wished Kaiser well in his industrial endeavors, he added a cautionary note: "There are problems in this mill....There are grievances here....These complaints should never be allowed to develop into grievances." Kaiser management could count on a friendly reception from top steelworker leadership, even if labor relations at the Fontana plant were not exactly perfect. Company pronouncements echoed the feel-good sentiments. According to KSC's 1956 annual report, "We believe that the right kind of employee relations is the very heart of the best things we accomplish....Our slogan, 'Together We Build,' must carry through all our daily associations."

From a national perspective, labor relations did look different at Fontana. The year 1946 is a great example. A national steel strike resulted from the difficult transition America endured as it lurched from a wartime to a peacetime economy; prices surged, and shortages of some goods emerged, while workers and companies tried to keep up. President Harry Truman unevenly lifted federal price controls after the war's end. Waves of strikes spread. A worried Truman invited Phil Murray and Ben Fairless to a meeting at the White House just four days before the strike deadline. The meeting only resulted in the two guests storming off, setting the stage for the western maverick Henry Kaiser to sweep in and steal the spotlight. Kaiser strode into the White House the following day and announced that his company would accept a compromise wage figure. He then immodestly proclaimed, "I have informed the President...that I have sufficient faith in this great nation to humbly take the lead in peace—as I did in war—in helping our people and our world." The entire spectacle was pure Kaiser. Phil Murray called on the nation's 750,000 steelworkers to strike, but Kaiser broke from the ranks of the steel industry and signed independently, as Kaiser-Frazer did with the auto industry strike. Kaiser so impressed the USWA leadership that they suggested steel plants still in government control after the war be given to men like Henry Kaiser to operate.

Kaiser Steel breaking from a united industry front and signing a contract in a media-hyped event became something of a pattern in the following years. In October 1949, steelworkers again hit the pavement as the industry contract expired without a resolution. Kaiser's four thousand steelworkers averted striking because, on October 5, KSC signed a contract with the union agreeing to have the company start to pay ten cents an hour for every hourly employee to support separate health and pension plans. With the signing of the 1949 contract, hourly KSC workers saw their health insurance become covered under the Kaiser Health Plan. As stories of strikes across the nation grabbed conspicuous media attention but skipped over Fontana, observers could think that there really was something different going on at Kaiser Steel.

The participation of the United States in the Korean War complicated the signing of the national 1952 steel industry contract; steel shortages brought

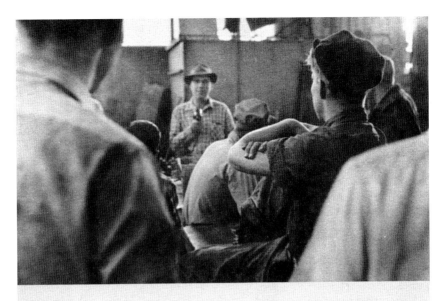

KAISER COMPANIES EMPLOYEE RELATIONS POLICIES

We believe that the right kind of employee relations is the very heart of the best things we accomplish.

Our slogan, "Together We Build," must carry through all our daily associations. Teamwork creates more opportunities for all, better understanding of each other, more security, and more of the satisfactions and good things of life. Teamwork is also required to satisfy our present customers and win new customers through timely delivery of quality products at competitive prices.

To maintain and improve this spirit of teamwork, Management employees must carry out their leadership responsibilities by conducting themselves in their daily relationships with their fellow employees with a genuine desire to secure their respect and loyalty. This can be accomplished only by consistent actions of helpfulness, understanding, fairness, and honesty.

Therefore, we believe it is our responsibility to our employees to:

1. Respect the dignity of each individual and recognize the importance of his job in achieving the continued growth and prosperity of the Company for the benefit of all.

2. Pay fair wages and salaries, supplemented by fair benefits for their services.

3. Make every effort to provide steady employment.

4. Encourage and assist employees in self-development and provide advancement opportunity for those who demonstrate ability and initiative.

5. Provide information on what the Company is doing, such as its growth, plans for the future, day-to-day problems and its accomplishments.

6. Provide a safe and suitably equipped place to work.

7. Resolve employees' problems with fairness and promptness in accordance with established procedures.

8. Deal fairly and respectfully with representatives of employees who have elected to be represented by a labor organization, observe the spirit as well as the letter of labor agreements and work sincerely to make the relationship of constructive benefit to the employees, the Union and the Company.

Employee relations were often highlighted in Kaiser Steel's annual reports, such as this one from 1956.

back some government regulation of vital materials, such as steel. Steel producers found doing business within the federal government's wartime price controls to be confining and used their narrowing profit margins as justification for rejecting the USWA's latest demands for wage increases. Labor wanted the new labor accord to include an 18.5-cent-per-hour wage hike, but the industry would not consider a substantial increase without the government allowing a $12-per-ton increase in the price of steel. With the war raging, President Truman argued that the nation faced a national emergency and the war effort would be severely compromised if steel production ceased. Truman had several options in dealing with this crisis, such as invoking the recently passed Taft-Hartley Act, which could end the strike. Turning away from the Taft-Hartley option, on April 8, Truman ordered the secretary of commerce to "seize" eighty-six steel plants around the nation in the name of the United States government and continue production. The presidential action sent steelworkers back to their jobs, but it did not solve the underlying labor disagreement. Amid a series of court injunctions and stays, the U.S. Supreme Court ultimately ruled Truman's action illegal, allowing the steelworkers to resume their strike. But what of Fontana? Following past practice, Kaiser Steel began negotiations with the industry, but after two months of participating in the industry front, the western maverick and a couple of other smaller companies pulled out and signed independently. Consequently, Kaiser Steel's 5,700 steelworkers never hit the pavement in the 1952 national strike. The 1952 annual report mentioned that there had been "no interruption of production at the Fontana plant" because of strikes, discussed the hundreds of thousands of dollars Kaiser management had plowed into the new company hospital, then concluded by saying, "Favorable living conditions in the Fontana area have contributed greatly to a stable working force. A large number of the employees own their own homes in what is predominantly an agricultural area with good schools and recreational facilities. These factors reflect high worker morale, good productivity for the plant." From issues of the *Snorter* printed during WWII through issues of the *Ingot* from the 1950s, holidays brought special greetings and recognition from Henry Kaiser, Bess Kaiser and others in the Kaiser Steel hierarchy, with headlines such as "Mrs. Kaiser Salutes You" and "Henry J. Kaiser's Tribute to Labor." A superficial reading of the Kaiser Steel story, such as the narrative coming from company literature, would suggest that the Fontana plant was a unique place of labor harmony.

A lack of strikes by Fontana's production workers authorized by United Steelworkers leadership did make the Kaiser plant unusual, but work stoppages, unsanctioned ones, did occur at Kaiser Steel nonetheless. Through the years, individual workers or small teams walked off the job in protest over one issue or another, as would happen at most any steel plant. There were many dozens of such isolated stoppages, in fact, but these isolated walkouts seldom had a broad impact on the operation of the entire steelworks. A couple of these unsanctioned so-called wildcat strikes, led by production and maintenance workers of USWA 2869, did close the plant completely, though.

Early in the morning on April 21, 1954, a handful of Kaiser steelworkers walked off their jobs. But this unauthorized (not sanctioned by the national USWA headquarters in Pittsburgh) work stoppage quickly enveloped the entire workforce, "except the smallest maintenance crew necessary to care for equipment," shuttering the entire plant. A newspaper in the neighboring city of Ontario reported that the men involved, machinists and an electrician, "were asked to move a 4 ½-ton motor, which union spokesmen said is a job usually done by forge and weld riggers." Arguing that Kaiser Steel management was adhering to the labor contract, the company statement of April 23 referred to contract wording, saying, "The Company, 'under no circumstances' shall consider the grievance of the four employees who refused to do the work assigned by their supervisor until the work stoppage is over." Furthermore, company officials were waiting for the United Steelworkers of America head office to enforce the contract and demand an end to the walkout. Job descriptions at the Fontana plant, like at all unionized steel plants, were meticulously defined and strictly followed. Exactly defining and protecting job descriptions was a major part of the process of creating a labor agreement in this era. In fact, it was a constant process, hashed out between workers and their immediate supervisors, discussed in concert with union reps and punctuated every few years by actual contract negotiations. For a worker to have a certain job classification meant having certain carefully articulated responsibilities and no others. Assuming this story was accurate as reported, if the steelworkers in question had obeyed their supervisor, they would have been "crossing crafts," performing a job other workers were trained for and contractually obligated to do. And this scenario—less than a half-dozen workers walking off the job, leading to facility-wide stoppage—becomes difficult to explain if the plant enjoyed the kind of labor harmony described by top leaders in labor and management.

But far away from labor conferences and meetings between corporate chiefs and national labor leaders, on the steel plant shop floor in Fontana, the causes for the walkout seemed to be widely acknowledged. Angry steelworkers assembled at Local 2869's Fontana headquarters, Thimmes Hall, on the afternoon the walkout began. Union local 2869 president Dave Walton charged that the larger issue "was an intended program to wear out the union....We feel that the company has abrogated the contract,

A local newspaper account of the December 1954 stoppage.

the company that workers would not show up to the plant the next day. Like the previous plant-wide stoppage months before at KSC, this strike originated from the Fontana shop floor.

Labor leaders were unsure how to proceed. That Sunday, Local 2869 president Dave Walton and area USWA official Lloyd Dayton each refused to comment on the strike, and Bill Brunton, who was a firebrand during the December wildcat strike, could not be reached for comment. The Steelworkers' International office found itself in the awkward and uncomfortable position of wanting to represent its members (like Bill Phebus) but also being bound to uphold its recently signed labor contract. Walking that tightrope delicately, the United Steelworkers issued a statement that expressed "complete sympathy with the employe [*sic*] discharged by the Kaiser Steel Corp." but still branded the strike "unauthorized" and urged workers to honor their contract.

Various forces came together quickly to resolve the stoppage. President Walton called a general meeting on Sunday night to discuss the strike and picked Fontana Junior High School's auditorium, a much larger venue than union headquarters at Thimmes Hall. On December 21, a crowd of 2,500 KSC employees packed the room, with hundreds more spilling out into the night. Taking the floor to speak, Walton defended Phebus's actions, calling on workers to "stand behind Billy—it might have been me or you." But from "upstairs" in Pittsburgh, Billy Brunton read a strongly worded letter from USWA president McDonald that called for the "illegal" strike to end immediately. The four-hour meeting climaxed with a secret vote on whether to continue to strike or return to work. In a rebuke to Walton and Phebus, workers voted to end the stoppage; no further vote breakdown was provided. Not surprisingly, Kaiser management felt vindicated by the vote. In an early draft of a letter intended to be released to workers, Jack Ashby interpreted the vote outcome as a "vast majority" of workers voicing a "clear repudiation of the irresponsible act of a few individuals who have brought harm to thousands of innocent persons." After the December stoppage, it appeared Kaiser management had lost patience with USWA Local 2869; the vote being "a public declaration by our employees that they want to live by the labor contract between their union and their company." Fontana's labor problems had begun to fester by the mid-1950s.

Underscoring the difficulty of implementing Henry J. Kaiser's rhetoric about the ease of translating the idea of labor peace into real labor peace on the shop floor, a third wildcat strike silenced the Kaiser steelworks just months later. In the KSC Ingot, that company stated that on September 26, 1955, it was necessary to cease operations at the steel plant due to a walkout of the railroad employees. For reasons unknown, someone allowed Southern Pacific employees to move railcars at the Kaiser plant, an action forbidden in the contract. Angry Kaiser Steel rail workers received no satisfaction when they confronted their supervisors, and their continued protestation led their bosses to send them home with disciplinary actions and without pay. Other KSC rail crews around the plant then responded by walking off their jobs. The departure of these key workers made continued plant operation impossible, so management closed the plant. Local leader Walton directed some (respectful) scorn to the famous industrialist Henry Kaiser when he said in a local paper, "Either Mr. Kaiser does not know that the policy which he spoke so highly of does not exist here in Fontana, or he did not mean what he said." The Fontana plant remained closed for several days.

And outside Local 2869's problems, problems existed between the company and its employees belonging to USWA Local 3677, Kaiser Steel's clerical and technical workers. During the ongoing closure, at 12:01 a.m. on October 1, 1955, the 347 employees in Fontana's smaller local of the United Steelworkers began a strike authorized by the Pittsburgh union headquarters when the company and labor could not resolve a pay dispute before the old contract covering these workers expired. This became the first authorized strike in KSC's thirteen-year history. This has remained largely unreported in other histories addressing Kaiser Steel, because 3677 was about one-tenth the size of 2869 and because steelworkers in Local 3677 did not have production jobs and thus had less visibility and legitimacy than "real" steelworkers. Adding to this "second class" status was the fact that USWA Local 3677 was composed mostly of women. And unlike the other plant-wide strikes at Kaiser, this first ever sanctioned strike concerned wages, a point on which KSC had always seemed generous. The starting pay rate for clerical workers at Fontana formed the primary stumbling block in signing the contract for Local 3677. Representatives for 3677 demanded that KSC raise the starting pay for clerical workers from $1.38 per hour to the industry standard of $1.58. The contract expired while negotiations continued, leading to the walkout, which sent these workers out to the pavement to join the 5,500 members of USWA Local 2869 already there. KSC's Industrial Relations Department conducted talks with the two locals separately and concurrently. When the company agreed to take back the rail workers and rip up the "white slips" issued to them for leaving their jobs, KSC's production and maintenance workers agreed to return to work on Sunday, October 9. Still, the plant remained silent, as members of 2869 voted to stay out as a show of solidarity with their union brothers and sisters in 3677. Then, in a sudden reversal of its position, on October 12, KSC management agreed to bump up the starting wages of office workers, which satisfied one union demand and brought the strike to an end. The steel mill roared back to life over the next few days, but weaknesses in the appearance of labor harmony were now evident.

The unrest at the Fontana plant suggests that as the company grew in the 1950s, the high-minded (and sincerely felt) speeches and adages of Henry J.

KAISER STEEL CORPORATION
ANNUAL REPORT · 1959

The impressive twenty-eight-story Oakland headquarters of the Kaiser business empire (steel, aluminum, auto, engineering, broadcasting, etc.), called Kaiser Center, opened in 1960.

Kaiser could not keep his steel operation out of hot water with its workers and their union. Now well into his sixties and newly remarried, Henry Kaiser was turning more of his attention to his new life in Hawaii and semiretirement. Edgar Kaiser also directed much of his executive responsibilities toward the other parts of the family empire (chemical, cement, engineering, automotive). But even if Henry and Edgar could have spent more of their time with the steel business, there is no guarantee that they could have forestalled the rising labor problems. Working out of Oakland, they might have been just as removed from the realities of the Fontana shop floor as Jack Ashby and other top KSC managers.

Chapter 4

KSC AND THE 1959 STRIKE

"ONLY 2% OF STEEL PRODUCTION BUT 98% OF THE INDUSTRY'S BRAINS"

Background to the Strike

The participation of Kaiser steelworkers in the nationwide 1959 strike had been in the making for years, although not all Kaiser Steel observers saw it coming. For example, one of Henry Kaiser's biographers, longtime KSC executive Al Heiner, called the stoppage the "implausible strike." Through the 1956 contract, after U.S. Steel and the other bigger firms argued, threatened, bluffed, maybe took a brief walkout or a protracted strike, then signed an agreement, Kaiser Steel workers and managers observed the proceedings from the sidelines with a cool detachment. Even if Kaiser Steel had representatives present at industry talks, the California-based company enjoyed an unusual flexibility with a later contract expiration date, known as a lag date. KSC pulled out of industry talks early if it wished, or it waited for the strike, then offered the industry package to its workers (or offered a package that was later adopted by the industry), addressed some local issues in the contract, then signed a strike-free deal. This special arrangement contributed tremendously to the absence of authorized strikes at Fontana. But the lag date also masked underlying tensions that existed at Fontana. Moving the termination date of the labor contract to the same date as the rest of the industry for the 1959 contract had a pivotal effect on Kaiser Steel's sanctioned strike-free history: it promptly ended.

A ladle of molten metal at the Fontana plant, 1957.

After the 1956 contact negotiations, leaders from the United Steelworkers of America and Kaiser Steel all agreed that the company should join industry-wide bargaining and share the same termination date for the next contract: June 30, 1959. In fact, by the mid-1950s, KSC managers came to believe that the union was using the lag date to their advantage in labor negotiations in order to make it harder for Kaiser managers to meet the challenge of controlling labor costs. One former Kaiser labor relations official called this alleged union practice "whipsawing" and cited it as a major reason why the company turned its back on its lag date in the 1950s. Henry and Edgar were more reluctant to cast their lot with the industry, but general manager Jack Ashby and others convinced the boardroom to change its approach. The United Steelworkers likewise came to favor Kaiser Steel abandoning the contract's lag date. According to a longtime USWA official, Cass Alvin, the union had originally felt that Kaiser Steel "needed [the lag date] because it was a new enterprising company that had a lot of adversaries within its own ranks in the steel industry." To protect this significant new source of jobs on the West Coast, a source that union leaders hoped would be a seed company creating other high-paying industrial jobs in the area, labor men wanted to give KSC a break, at least until its success was assured.

For the 1959 contract negotiations, Kaiser Steel committed itself to standing with a large and powerful consortium of steel producers, some ninety steel firms bound together by the contract. To expedite the negotiation process and maintain the advantage that came from speaking with one voice, steel firms formed the "Big Twelve," a group of America's largest dozen steel outfits. These twelve companies accounted for about 90 percent of American steelmaking capacity, although giants U.S. Steel and Bethelehem Steel overwhelmingly dominated steel output. They held talks at the famous Waldorf Astoria Hotel in New York City, far from any major steel production. KSC sent Jack Ashby and members of KSC's Industrial Relations Department to the meetings to represent it among the Big Twelve. Edgar Kaiser also spent considerable time at the Waldorf through the summer of 1959. Both union and management sent their big guns to represent them in the contract discussions. Individual companies, including Kaiser Steel, still held talks with the union unilaterally at other locations to discuss issues of local interest, but the industry-wide talks held at the Waldorf attracted the lion's share of the nation's attention.

For the first time in the company's history, KSC's company newspaper became an industry and company mouthpiece in the months leading up to a contract settlement. From 1958 through 1959, the *Ingot* printed articles with titles like "Employment Costs Up $680 Million in Steel Industry Since '56 Pact" and "Steel Industry Fringe Benefits Set New Record." The articles reminded Kaiser Steel workers that their wages had increased substantially over the years, with straight time wages more than doubling from 1947 through 1958. The company was trying to convince workers that it was not in the position to increase its costs; it simply could not afford such generosity.

But did the industry make an honest argument when it claimed that it could not afford to pay its workers more? As a whole, the steel industry made immense profits in the postwar period. The industry production leader, U.S. Steel, also led the way in sales and profits by a massive margin in the 1950s. The company boasted of profits totaling $184.3 million in 1951 and reached its peak yearly profit level for the 1950s of $419.5 million in 1957. Although not even in the same ballpark with U.S. Steel and Bethlehem's performance, Kaiser Steel earned a profit every year from 1951 through 1958. In 1951, its first year as a publicly traded company, Kaiser Steel Corporation earned $7.5 million, and its yearly profits peaked for the decade in 1956 at $23.6 million. And for the decade 1951–59, KSC posted a cumulative profit of $91.3 million. Henry Kaiser silenced the pundits who predicted that he would lose his shirt making steel, but the profits earned were dwarfed by the costly continuous expansion the plant had undergone since 1942, not to mention the most recent $214 expansion program. With its smaller profit levels, high debt-to-profit ratio and imperative to build an all-new facility at Fontana, as opposed to updating an older facility, arguably Kaiser Steel had a convincing position when it claimed that it could not afford substantial increases in its labor costs.

The United Steelworkers of America fielded an aggressive media blitz of its own, zeroing in on the steel industry's huge profits to justify demands for gains for workers in the next contract. Sometimes labeling such earnings as the "billion-dollar bundle," the union charged that the increased wages labor wanted could be easily afforded by these wealthy industrial giants and that increased wages for the nation's 750,000 steelworkers would actually boost mass purchasing power and charge the nation's economic engine.

While labor and industry feuded in the media for public support, preliminary high-level meetings between the parties began in early April 1959. A letter issued by the Big Twelve set the tone for the talks—and for the public relations war. The letter was ostensibly written for David McDonald, but the industry group actually had its sights set on rank-and-file steelworkers and the public at large. Stating the problem in terms that people could readily understand, the industry organ reminded readers that "among the problems which concern thinking people in America today, few are more talked about than or are of greater interest than inflation, unemployment, and mounting competition from abroad." Avoiding a strike in 1956 by conceding to labor's demands had proved costly to the steel industry, so management had plenty of motivation to stand fast against labor's demands for more increases in wages and benefits in the 1959 contract talks.

But couched within these messages that focused on the merits of and problems with increasing wages and benefits were small and easily overlooked references to an even thornier issue facing labor and industry. The problem lurking under the surface, which would eventually stall the talks, was interpreting "work rules" at steel plants. The broad category of rights and powers referred to as work rules embraced privileges, job descriptions, work crew compositions, some disciplinary actions and other aspects of work that had been recognized by management and largely determined by labor. These "past practices" remained a place where labor could exert some real autonomy in the workplace environment, and organized labor dug in its heels to defend them in 1959. On the other side of the issue, management began to articulate a strong desire to gain the power to revise past practices more in its favor, such as allowing management to dictate the composition of work crews and perhaps to use new labor-saving machinery in order to lower labor costs. Control over the shop floor actually became the axis on which the 1959 strike revolved, even if this fact surfaced in the press rather gradually. On April 30, USWA's Wage Policy Committee issued its list of demands to the steel industry for the 1959 contract, which included a significant wage increase, continuation of the cost-of-living provision, improvement of the Sunday premium, establishment of a Saturday premium, a hike in the holiday premium, an increase in the number of paid holidays, improved vacation benefits, improved pensions, expanded social insurance programs and increased shift premiums and severance allotments. In the spring of 1959, the union still had a rather vague and evolving list of demands. But on one issue there would be no equivocation: retaining the "past practice" of interpreting work rules.

Formal negotiations at the Waldorf between the Big Twelve and the USWA commenced in May 1959. The two sides met regularly without much progress, and by June, Big Twelve negotiators felt the need to articulate the industry's positions to union members and the general public. This evolving set of positions was beginning to focus more sharply on one aspect of the labor deal. The industry presented an early version of its positions in a letter addressed to David J. McDonald dated June 10. By this point, the industry voiced a willingness to grant modest increases in wages and benefits, as long as they were "non-inflationary"; the generosity of the 1956 deal could not be repeated. While there was some softness on wage and benefit issues, the industry group was not flexible on another issue: work rules. In that June document, the industry team insisted that management have more control over wildcat strikes, work scheduling and establishing seniority, and insisted

The motto "Together We Build" was commonly seen in company publications, commemorative jewelry and plaques in the first half of the company's history.

on the "necessity to revise paragraph 2-B," a critical issue ignored in previous industry demands released to the press.

The problematic 2-B part of the contract creating the showdown, entitled "Local Working Conditions," formed labor's "line in the sand" in this strike and was a prime target of industry negotiators. Section 2-B became part of the steel contract in 1947. In the 1956 contract, which was lapsing in 1959, Section 2-B comprised six paragraphs that protected the "specific practices or customs which reflect detailed application of the subject matter within the scope of wages, hours of work, or other conditions of employment and include local agreements, written or oral, on such matters." A complete listing of every such relevant task at something as complicated as a steel plant would be mind-boggling, which is reflected in 2-B's admission that "it is recognized that it is impractical to set forth in this Agreement all of these working conditions, which are of a local nature only, or to state specifically in this Agreement which of these matters should be changed or eliminated." Such vagueness needed to be used to keep the contract from taking up hundreds or even thousands of pages, but it also left the door wide open for disagreement between labor and management. If management wanted to consolidate, eliminate or change in any way a recognized job or accepted practice of a job, whether or not those jobs or practices were clearly defined in the contract, it could do so, but it had to defend its action to the union. Steelworkers clung tenaciously to these restraints imposed upon managerial prerogative. Steelworkers supported 2-B and wanted there to be more protection of past practices; management wanted the wording in 2-B changed to give them more "right to manage." For example, at the Kaiser plant, as well as others in the 1950s, locomotive crews had a fireman on board the train at all times because this practice extended back to when steam-powered locomotives required a man dedicated to dealing with the firebox. Yet firemen continued to be a fixture in the crews operating diesel-electric locomotives, although there were no flames for firemen to attend to. Management looked at such practices as having firemen in diesel locomotives as examples of "featherbedding." Labor saw keeping firemen in diesels as insurance that crews would have enough skilled people on board to safely and effectively operate the machine.

Sensing encroachment on its hotly defended turf, labor rejected the industry overture sternly, and McDonald charged that the new focus of industry's negotiations on weakening work rules was an attempt to "break the Union." The industry's new stance had the unintended result of mobilizing labor to fight as little else could have. McDonald said that the industry's June statement concerning work rules had, overnight, transformed union members from "apathetic to the negotiations" and "generally fat and comfortable" to "fighting mad." By June 1959, as the contract deadline approached, the two sides seemed to be moving further apart.

In a letter dated June 23, David McDonald informed President Dwight Eisenhower that the steel labor negotiations had stalled and that a national steel strike appeared imminent. Hoping for some help from Ike to prevent a stoppage, McDonald suggested that the government step into the process, perhaps setting up "a fact-finding board to hear the evidence." Eisenhower responded to McDonald two days later, encouraging him to continue talking with industry representatives but rejecting McDonald's call for forming a new federal panel. The ideologically conservative Ike reminded McDonald that the federal government did have an agency that stood ready to serve if called: the Federal Mediation and Conciliation Service (FMCS). Neither the industry nor the union had asked to use the agency at that point, but Ike noted that the FMCS "stands ready at any time to assist the parties to reach agreement." Because of steel's huge contribution to the nation's economy, Americans followed the daily report reporting on contract talks.

Working every day and long into the night, negotiators eyed the new July 15 deadline with grim determination while steelworkers, steel firm managers and many other interested parties prepared for the strike. Steel-consuming companies stockpiled the vital metal during the spring and early summer. Like steelworkers nationwide, Kaiser Steel employees kept abreast of the contract situation. United Steelworkers Local 2869 set up a strike committee to prepare for what was looking like a certain strike. One former Kaiser steelworker in the tin mill, Mildred Foust, remembered the slow rollout of the stoppage: "I saw the strike coming." Workers took note of the sudden increased production rate, the stories of stalled talks and the warnings from union leaders to prepare for hard times. Foust knew the signs of an impending strike: "The union would tell you, 'Put a can away, and a quarter,'" she recalled.

The night before the extended contract deadline expired, Local 2869 leaders called a special meeting at the Fontana union headquarters that attracted about 1,500 Kaiser workers. National headlines reported that the steel talks had broken down, leading observers to predict a certain strike in steel, a sentiment widely held in Fontana. "If anybody says you got friends in the Kaiser Corp.," USWA official Harold Rasmussen told the throng of KSC workers jammed into Thimmes Hall on July 13, "he's been smoking marijuana." Rasmussen charged that "Mr. Kaiser may own this corporation but it's controlled and operated by the Wall Street bankers." Whipping up the crowd into an anti-management fever, KSC worker, grievance man and labor activist Ronald "Ronnie" Bitonti called another Kaiser negotiator a "hatchet man using methods similar to Al Capone in an attempt to get us to break off negotiations."

Neither labor nor industry had highlighted the work rules issue in their press releases leading up to the strike. In part, this silence reflects the slippery and confusing nature of work rules and the corresponding difficulty of relating them to the public. The union faced the challenge of explaining section 2-B to worker families. One of Local 2869's negotiators at the Fontana talks, pipe mill worker Timon "Curley" Covert, remembered organizing a meeting because defending 2-B presented "a kind of difficult thing to explain, so we held a special union meeting for…the women, women only; wives, sisters, cousins.…We passed out as the people came in a white slip of paper to every tenth person that came through the door. And as we started getting into the meeting and explaining it, drew it all out, then at one point in there we said,

'Every woman that has a white slip, hold it up. If you look around you will see how many of you, your husbands, your brother, or someone, is going to be out of a job'" if Kaiser management had its way with watering down section 2-B.

THE STRIKE

Late in the afternoon on Tuesday, July 14, the order came from the United Steelworkers headquarters in Pittsburgh via teletype to waiting union members in Fontana. Barring a highly unlikely last-minute settlement, all union members would cease work that evening at midnight. Not only was this KSC's first sanctioned strike involving its production and maintenance workers, but it threatened to be a particularly long strike, too, as the two sides remained so far apart on issues and seemed so resistant to compromise. President Eisenhower offered a rare optimistic forecast for success in the talks as the strike loomed. "I am confident," the president told the press, "that with good will on both sides of the bargaining table agreement can be reached without undue delay." David McDonald might not have personally poured or rolled steel in the postwar years, but he still heard workers' frustration with managerial practices and the overwhelming desire of members to strike. Labor historian David Brody was probably correct when he concluded that "McDonald, no enthusiast of industrial war, probably could have held back the steelworkers only at his own peril."

Although the 1959 steel strike became the longest strike in American steel industry history, it did not bring the numerous bloody confrontations between workers and management seen in some of America's great strikes of decades past. Through American history, industrial strikes regularly resulted in violence, injuries and death. As rationale for hiring goons as strikebreakers (or "guards"), stockpiling weapons, spying on union members and committing other nefarious acts, steel industry managers offered as their defense the protection of private property. The federal government legitimized labor unions in the 1930s, especially with passage of the National Industrial Recovery Act's section 7a in 1933, followed by the Wagner Act in 1935, and brought about what David Brody called "workplace rule of law." By the time of the steel strike of 1959, instead of hiring Pinkertons to crush unions and their organizing efforts, steel companies had industrial relations departments dedicated to smoothing out the relationship between an organized workforce and management. Similar conditions prevailed in Fontana. The USWA International headquarters handed down strike instructions encouraging peaceful behavior. Local officials were responsible for enforcing these rules at the plant gates. Local 2869 president Joe Zeno formed and led the strike committee at Fontana. The committee oversaw the continuous picketing of the plant gates and monitored the making and use of placards to ensure they followed regulations. Strikers who pulled strike detail received food and coffee but could not have or use alcohol on the picket line. Strikers walking the line allowed a handful of Fontana's 7,500 employees to pass, like members of KSC management, several hundred members of Local 2869 on special stand-by crews that maintained delicate equipment and members of USWA Local 3677, KSC's clerical and technical workers. Local 3677 did not walk out on strike because their contract had not expired, so they crossed the line only with the permission, and grudging approval, of picketing 2869 members. Walking through a picket line was highly stressful for strikers. Picketers really serve several functions by their actions; picketers walked in front of the Kaiser gates to broadcast their displeasure with management, to prevent business as usual, to keep out any replacement workers and to dissuade any less-than-fully-committed union members from reporting to work. After all, the point of a strike is to put economic pressure on the company by stopping production. Tin mill worker Tom Rabone remembered the firm dedication that those on picket duty brought to strikes in Fontana, saying, "They were some tough cookies! If there was a walk-out and you got to the gate and they told you not to work… you better not go to work!"

The first formal local talks for the 1959 contract held in Fontana took place in the plant's labor relations conference room on June 3, 1959, weeks before the strike began. Over the following four-and-a-half months, the two sides met numerous times, usually in that Fontana conference room but occasionally elsewhere, even in New York City. Kaiser Steel's team invited labor to begin the proceedings by airing its list of demands; it presented sixty. This list of demands, to which labor added a few as time passed, drove the discussions. Among other requests, Kaiser Steel employees wanted to form a joint labor-management committee to oversee garnishment of wages arising out of disciplinary action, a cap placed on how long Employee Performance Slips (a disciplinary action) stayed active, realignment of how seniority was determined in coke oven crews, the creation of a new job description for electronic repairmen, changing of tires by members of garage personnel only and the plant-wide standardization of starting and ending times for shift schedules.

In the local talks, a few points received quick approval by the company. Local 2869's Keith Geisert requested that management OK chairs being installed in several control pulpits around the plant so operating men could sit while overseeing their work. Curly Covert said, "Our Superintendent periodically goes over our engines and throws all of our improvised seats out." Clearly frustrated, Covert wondered aloud why something as basic as having chairs so men don't have to sit on the floor had to be negotiated. Company representative Bob Likens concurred, saying, "That's what I'm wondering. We will take a look at it."

The company presented its own short list of demands. This list raised the hackles of workers. Just like steel firms across America, Kaiser Steel managers wanted to rein in labor costs by gaining more control over work rules and job responsibilities, some written down and some simply recognized over time through past practice. Management had isolated a handful of these unwritten work rules plant-wide, and they presented the list to labor representatives at the July negotiations. For example, KSC management demanded that the position of utility man in the pipe mill be eliminated and that inspectors be present when rolls were changed in the forty-six-inch slabbing mill. Kaiser managers had determined that these positions were not needed, although men were paid to hold them. Therefore, the company looked upon these jobs as examples of "featherbedding." When Bob Likens proposed that the forty-six-inch mill utility man position be liquidated, Curly Covert could not restrain himself. He later remembered, "I broke out laughing! And I says, 'Go ahead…take him off. They can have it. They can't run that mill out there 15 minutes without him.'" In spite of whatever Henry Kaiser might have said about the simplicity of labor relations—that having men of good faith in place was all it took to prevent work stoppages and achieve labor harmony—Kaiser Steel company negotiators took a different tack in the 1959 contract talks.

Through the summer months, the talks in New York and Fontana brought no progress. Growing more impatient with the lack of movement, President Eisenhower wrote to labor and industry leaders in early September, urging the two sides to begin "intensive, uninterrupted, good-faith bargaining." Ike chastised, "I have seen far more difficult problems than the steel dispute resolved in far less time by people who spoke different languages and had diverse backgrounds." When the letter achieved no positive results, Eisenhower called a group of steel industry and labor representatives to the White House for a personal meeting with him on September 30. The president made clear to those in attendance that he would not rule out using

West Receives High Share of Steel Imports

The far west accounts for a relatively high percentage of the total steel imported into the United States, according to a recent Kaiser steel report. In 1958 the seven western states accounted for 9.2 per cent of the national steel market and for 19 per cent of national steel imports.

Western imports, in line with the national situation, have been increasing from a 150,000 ton annual average from 1951 through 1957, to 324,000 tons in 1958, and to an annual rate of about 450,000 tons in early 1959.

The relatively greater role of foreign steel in the western mar-

SMOG HIDDEN—Somewhere in the central mass of smog pictured above lies the Kaiser Steel Plant. Almost half a billion dollars in plant and property lies idle on the 20th day of the strike at high noon—completely obscured by polluted air drifting in from remote sources.

Construction and Repair Projects Payroll Loss Told

Kaiser Steel last week denied the charge by a local Union leader that construction work could be done more cheaply during the strike than when the mill is operating.

Earl S. Reynolds, director of Public Relations for Kaiser Steel, said: "The Company tried to negotiate with the Union to allow outside construction workers to cross the picket lines and enter the plant to complete building of six new soaking pits and to reline a blast furnace. The Union has refused the request, according to the Union leader's statement, on the claim that the Company could do the job more cheaply during a

The company frequently addressed the plant's contribution to regional smog, as seen here during the 1959 strike; the plant closed, but bad air quality remained.

Taft-Hartley, a 1947 act of Congress that curtails the power of labor unions and allows the U.S. president to intervene in strikes, in the very near future. He pleaded with the two parties to resume a genuine dialogue, and while talks began again, they failed to achieve success. On October 3, in last-ditch talks, the industry made its final offer to labor: it would give a fifteen-cent-per-hour pay hike over a two-year period, but it still wanted to scale back the working conditions language in 2-B, and it refused to include a cost-of-living clause in the contract. The union rejected any tampering with working conditions language and demanded substantially more pay and benefits gains than the industry was willing to agree to: thirty-five to forty cents over three years. The work rules problem had become an impasse in the talks.

By the fall of 1959, steel labor and steel management were definitely feeling the high cost of the long stoppage. Workers scrambled to pay bills without their regular paychecks coming in, while managers looked at a swelling sea of red ink in their ledgers. Local 2869 passed out emergency aid and spread around limited moneymaking opportunities to as many members as possible. Since Kaiser Steel's furnaces needed to be carefully banked to prevent damage from inactivity, the Local had about seven hundred men working a few hours a week to maintain the well-being of the facilities. In order to help minimize some of the pain of the strike, about 20 percent of the gross earnings of those lucky enough to be working part time at the plant went right into the union welfare fund. The welfare fund, in turn, fed into projects like a voucher system. The Local issued vouchers to members to pay for groceries and utility bills from August, and by early October, all these vouchers totaled some $40,000. About one-third of all Kaiser Steel's striking workers had applied for the vouchers. The sheer number of the applicants swamped the fund, despite the International kicking in an additional $10,000. Facing continued demand for help, Local 2869 officials approached the San Bernardino County welfare office. Swallowing his pride, Local 2869's vice president Herbert Saltz explained to the local press that union welfare funds were "depleted" and that "we're not asking for anything any other citizen is not entitled to" in obtaining county assistance. To Saltz's dismay, the county rejected 2869's pleas, citing several reasons. County officials ruled out payments to any workers as long as alternate sources, such as the Local welfare fund, were still available, and as long as steelworkers could find something—anything—else to do (a union official admitted to the press that it "would be difficult to get the skilled men to take any job, say grape picking"). "No county in the state is able to cope with this large a problem under present welfare rules," explained a San Bernardino County welfare official.

While the Local did its best to rustle up support for its members, most workers had to forage on their own to earn money. Skilled men, like welders, machinists and electricians, could take their skills to construction sites, machine shops and contractors, where they could land good part-time jobs. But most striking Kaiser steelworkers who lacked these skills had to accept whatever modest opportunity they could get.

As Kaiser steelworkers welded at machine shops and milked cows, by the autumn months, Kaiser Steel's balance sheets began to register the very heavy costs of the strike. The steel industry did not enjoy the strongest of years in 1958 anyway. In 1958, KSC posted a disappointing $5.4 million profit on sales of over $181 million but, through the first six months of 1959, earned $10.2 million on sales of $147 million, most of this coming from last-minute stockpiling by strike-worried customers. However, the work stoppage completely wiped out even this modest recovery. Kaiser Steel lost $17.6 million in the last half of 1959, resulting in a total deficit of $7.4 million for the year on sales of $201.9 million. Kaiser managers had hoped that, in 1959, the company would be reaping increased operational efficiency. Blindsiding management was yet another factor that drove down earnings in 1959: increased competition from new steel suppliers. Kaiser Steel officials had begun to notice the growing market penetration of Belgian, Australian, German and Japanese manufacturers prior to 1959, especially in profitable small-diameter pipe. Foreign producers took almost one-third of KSC's western market in that product in 1958—and priced their pipe at thirty dollars less per ton than Kaiser—but the vacuum in U.S. production in 1959 opened the floodgates for imported steel products. What's more, the western states market attracted a higher percentage of imports than other parts of America. Kaiser Steel simply could not tolerate the flow of red ink as long or as easily as its larger competitors could. Kaiser's cash levels were too low, its debt too high and its profits too meager to stay closed for very long. Therefore, in the fall of 1959, certain elements within Kaiser Steel's corporate leadership began to rethink their loyalty to the Big Twelve.

The trigger that forced Kaiser Steel's hand regarding its role in the Big Twelve came from the White House. Fed up with the inability of steel labor and management to resolve their differences, Dwight Eisenhower announced on October 9 that he would force a resolution in the struggle through use of the Taft-Hartley Act. Ike's famous temper had been piqued. Eisenhower finally fell back on the powers given him by Taft-Hartley and directed the U.S. attorney general to obtain a court injunction to end the strike. The Taft-Hartley Act can force striking workers back to work by suspending the strike for an eighty-day "cooling off" period while the parties negotiate under the careful eye of the Federal Conciliation and Mediation Service. Neither steel labor nor management wanted Eisenhower to pick this option, and so few were surprised when the United Steelworkers appealed the injunction (on the grounds that Taft-Hartley was unconstitutional). Edgar Kaiser believed that forcing men back to work would only poison any hope for an amicable settlement and torpedo future goodwill communication with labor. He would do just about whatever needed to be done to avoid that scenario. By the fall of 1959, Henry and Edgar Kaiser, both of whom had little stomach for prolonged labor conflict, were itching to break out of the box in which the Big Twelve had kept them. By the mid-1950s, Henry J. was increasingly disconnected from his far-flung operations on the mainland, so son Edgar kept him abreast of developments in New York through daily phone calls to his home in Hawaii. According to a speech later made by Jack Ashby, as soon as it appeared that Ike would impose Taft-Hartley, Edgar "clarified his position with the steel industry, stating that before Kaiser Steel would take its people through the compulsion of Taft-Hartley, we would have to take another look at our position with respect to industry-wide bargaining." Rumors began to spread in the press of secret meetings between Edgar

Kaiser and union representatives, which both the company and the union flatly denied. Denials aside, the rumors were true. One union official remembers having to cover for his boss, USWA District 38 director "Charlie Smith, [who] was going around with Edgar Kaiser…in private planes." With Kaiser's loyalty to the united steel industry openly being discussed, U.S. Steel's chairman of the board, Roger Blough, met directly with Edgar; a Kaiser Steel departure could initiate an exodus of other steel firms, ceding the victory to labor, which "was put to Mr. Kaiser with considerable fervor." Kaiser fessed up that yes, he had been speaking with labor figures. Blough wanted him to stop. But Kaiser would not be bullied by the president of America's steel giant. Edgar, while agreeing to stand with industry on the one hand, on the other hand refused to break off communication with two specific labor figures, USWA president McDonald and legal council Arthur Goldberg. Edgar argued that it was a practical consideration, as Kaiser Industries had a steel company and an aluminum company that both had to sign contracts with the USWA, so those communication lines needed to remain open. Knowing that Kaiser Steel had reached its breaking point, David McDonald did an "end run" around Jack Ashby and confronted Edgar Kaiser directly, as had Blough. McDonald invited Edgar (but not Ashby) to his hotel room and then laid out his idea that Kaiser Steel break away from the Big Twelve with a direct "Edgar, let's break this thing open." Edgar did not dismiss the idea out of hand, but he told McDonald that he had to run specifics past his father first. Seizing the momentum, McDonald beat Edgar to the punch, immediately calling his friend Henry with the idea that Kaiser Steel sign an independent deal with the union. Henry J. agreed with McDonald that the strike had lasted far too long and that there had to be some kind of deal that they could cut. Henry instructed Edgar to serve as point man for the settlement, which the younger Kaiser agreed to be, but he did so largely without the support of either Jack Ashby (who still sat on the steel policy committee, which negotiated with the USWA) or the KSC industrial relations department. So the move by Kaiser Steel to leave the strike was made independently of the company's labor relations "team," not to mention the Big Twelve. Referring to the meeting in which he had to tell Blough and other steel company leaders that Kaiser Steel was breaking industry ranks, after pledging at least some degree of loyalty to them just days before, Kaiser reflected, "I don't think I ever had a tougher thing to do." In that meeting, Kaiser tried to get other steel leaders to find some kind of compromise with labor, but he failed to move them. Some were quite angry with Kaiser, one calling him "a traitor to America" and another a "socialist." On Sunday, October 24, Edgar Kaiser broke the news to his friend James Reston of the *New York Times*: the next day, Kaiser Steel Corporation would sign a unilateral contract with the United Steelworkers of America, ending its participation in the national steel strike after 104 days. Reston called his article "Mutiny in the Waldorf." The press picked up the story and broadcast it to the nation.

Back in Southern California, news of a strike settlement hit the press like a tsunami. Local newspapers blared banner headlines with messages like "KAISER AGREES TO SIGN." Local contract talks could be quickly pushed through to fruition if the New York negotiations reached their conclusion. Everyone waited for confirmation of a deal in New York. When the word came down from Edgar Kaiser and David McDonald on Monday that Kaiser Steel's 7,500 striking workers would return to work, relieved steelworkers on picket detail at the plant gates burned their strike placards. Both Local 2869 and 3677 would be getting brand-new contracts at the same time. The relief, even glee, among employees to be returning to work was easily visible and probably unanimous.

Kaiser Steel had once again broken ranks with the steel industry and signed a deal with the Steelworkers Union—only this time, the two sides agreed on a deal with some issues resolved but a surprising number left unresolved. In return, the signers agreed to a contract lasting only twenty months, expiring June 30, 1961, which would allow either one or both parties out of a disagreeable settlement. And most importantly for workers, there would be no changes made to the 2-B clause of the contract regarding

'MEET THE PRESS' . . .
(Continued from page 5)

Mr. Kaiser: Well, I think that the industry must take a step to solve what's been going on. The country cannot stand this continual period . . . we run up to a deadline and then we have a strike.

Q. Is the way to do it to give labor a larger voice in management?

Mr. Kaiser: I don't think you're talking about a larger voice in labor. I think it's a mutual problem. That is the fundamental difference, I guess, between Kaiser and the rest of industry. I think you have to do it that way.

Q. They say it's just a beginning toward a corporate state.

Mr. Kaiser: Well, I'm not so sure that's so. If you and I are doing something because we mutually agreed to it, I think we will do it a little better than we will if we've done it either because I have a unilateral power or you do.

Q. Makes the Union stronger and stronger.

Mr. Kaiser: Well, if the Union gains responsibility with strength, that is to the asset of the country.

Q. Well, Mr. Kaiser, you have been on the inside of these negotiations now for some time. Can you tell us what you believe

The *Ingot* featured a transcript and some photos of Edgar Kaiser's interview on the high-profile TV show *Meet the Press*.

work rules. Indeed, three things made the Kaiser Steel settlement significant: Kaiser pulled out of the Big Twelve and signed on its own, 2-B remained in the contract unchanged, and two committees were created that tackled thorny issues such as the introduction of more automation into production, defining work rules and sharing the profits of the corporation with employees. The first committee, a joint management-labor group, would discuss primarily nonwage issues. The committee's creators hoped the new group could diffuse problems concerning work rules and worker displacement due to new technology. Steelworkers faced a constant threat to their job security through the introduction of new technology, a situation faced by workers all over the country. The KSC-USWA accord provided that the joint committee be able to reach settlement of these issues only by mutual agreement; no company or union steamrolling over things would be allowed. Kaiser Steel had a modest history of breaking new ground in labor relations since its inception in 1942, and the small steel plant was more vulnerable to the economic fallout associated with strikes than its larger eastern competitors. This portion of the contract appealed to KSC managers because it promised to reduce the frequency of costly work stoppages and grievances by allowing the company to introduce money-saving technology more easily and solve other labor-related problems.

A second committee, made up of three elements, registered the lion's share of the public attention. Just the makeup of the committee made it controversial. In this tripartite group, labor and management were joined by members of the public in discussions and decisions made on "developing a long-range plan for the equitable sharing of future economic progress between stockholders, employees, and the public." Inviting labor to the table to discuss a company's economic planning was radical enough, but the 1959 plan also called for members of the public, named from a short list of people who had experience in labor relations and finance, to participate in creating a new system by which the company would share some greater part of its economic success, or "fruits," as it was commonly stated. Having members of the public and union members sit on the committee also implied that these parties would have access to the company's ledgers, because they would have to know some of Kaiser Steel's costs to formulate this fruits-sharing plan. Members within the labor movement had been asking for industry to "open its books" for several decades by 1959, and to the shock of some steel industry leaders, Kaiser Steel management appeared to be relenting on this point. Decades later, KSC's Mark Anthony revealed, "We had been working on various possible plans, and they just did not develop overnight."

Likewise, the union had been working with "Scanlon Plans" that had found a small measure of acceptance in steel, rubber, paper and other industries. While there was no single formula for Scanlon Plans, they generally worked by passing along a proportion of economic savings to the company from a reduction in costs in relation to profits; that was the seed of the Kaiser-USWA plan.

Kaiser Steel, really something of a Lilliputian in the industry, suddenly became front-page news with its settlement. Soon after the KSC-USWA settlement hit the newswires, the *Ingot* boasted that "swarms of newspaper, radio, television and motion picture newsreel men descended upon the plant as the West's largest producer captured the news headlines of the nation." On November 1, the television network NBC invited Edgar Kaiser to discuss his company's settlement on their popular news program *Meet the Press*. Kaiser betrayed little new or "inside" information in the interview, and he maintained his loyalty to the "non-inflationary" mantle of the Big Twelve generally. The interviewers treated Kaiser as if he was somehow more insightful, flexible or farsighted than his competitors still out on strike. Asked one interviewer, "Mr. Kaiser, some folks say that you represent only 2% of steel production but 98% of the industry's brains. Is that right?" Edgar thanked the man, then politely admitted with a chuckle, "I don't think that's right." For a brief period, Kaiser Steel and, to an extent, Edgar Kaiser were darlings of the popular media and in the esoteric world of labor relations. Edgar's face and words appeared in trade magazines, television programs and national newspapers like the *New York Times*, *Los Angeles Times*, and *Wall Street Journal*. Leaving Jack Ashby and the KSC Labor Relations Department—and even his father, in his tropical island retirement—on the sidelines, Edgar rapidly rose as the most prominent member of Kaiser Steel top management during the strike. As it turned out, the rest of America's steelworkers went back to work a few weeks after the KSC-USWA deal, steel management agreed to a pretty generous economic package and—something with more of a possible KSC stamp on it—the industry agreed to participate in a joint union/industry Human Relations Committee. McDonald and influential legal advisor (and future U.S. secretary of labor) Arthur Goldberg had been backing some kind of increased industry/labor cooperation for some time; now it was going to happen. In this 1959 settlement, Edgar Kaiser had maneuvered himself and his company to take the most provocative and prominent place in American industry that it would ever have.

With the open-ended deadline for the committee stretching out the delivery of a finished Long-Range Sharing Plan, the company and union nonetheless had to sign labor contracts before the plan was ready. In 1961, with no plan in sight, the company and union quickly signed another brief "Band-Aid" contract, lasting one year and expiring on June 30, 1962. When the exact same situation for contract renewal presented itself a year later, negotiators worked out another stopgap agreement. Edgar Kaiser applied pressure to Fontana's labor relations personnel to ensure a quick and trouble-free contract signing. In an interoffice memo dated April 26, 1962, KSC labor relations official Walter Farrell instructed his people, "In accordance with Edgar's recent request...increased emphasis...[will] be placed on our over-all objective of commencing and concluding our negotiations as far in advance of contract expiration dates as possible."

After nearly three years of secretive work, on January 11, 1963, the committee finally released the Long-Range Sharing Plan for consideration. Upon first inspection, the plan seemed to satisfy the demands of labor. For one thing, the plan promised workers that they would benefit more from the company's financial success, a central point for labor. The LRSP gave participating workers a share of savings realized at the Fontana steel plant by any means, from use of new, efficient technology on the shop floor to lowering energy costs. If the company cut the number of jobs to lower operating costs, those savings would be distributed. This clause of the plan might have appeared on its face to be unacceptable to labor, but the LRSP made job loss more acceptable because it provided for laid-off workers to go into a job reserve for reassignment. Empowered by the plan, Kaiser management could be more aggressive about cost cutting using new technology and about deleting jobs, if it adhered to the guidelines of section 2-B protecting past practices. Labor scored a major victory by keeping the language of 2-B intact in the labor contract. Through a very complicated (and constantly changing) process, the committee determined the cost of buying energy, purchasing materials and a plethora of other factors in Fontana's operating costs. These costs formed the base from which savings in these areas over subsequent months, if there were any, could be compared. A percentage of the savings realized, 32.5 percent, would be passed along to workers. Thus, workers received bonus checks not necessarily if the company posted higher profits or sales but rather if the company generated higher savings as defined in the Sharing Plan contract. All wage workers who participated in the plan received these checks, whether they worked in offices or in the open hearth furnace department; the exact amount was pegged to their take-home pay.

Therefore, participating workers in higher job classifications with higher pay would receive more bonus pay than persons in lower-classification jobs with lower take-home pay. And just to make sure that workers did not get soaked with a bad bonus plan, all participating workers were guaranteed "wage and benefit increases equal to or better than what might be granted by the rest of the industry." To implement the plan, it had to be approved by a majority of participating Kaiser Steel workers in a vote.

Not all Kaiser Steel employees would receive coverage under the new plan if implemented, though. Nonparticipating employees were salaried workers (management) and those hourly workers who already participated in Kaiser's ongoing bonus system: incentive pay. These hourly workers had been augmenting their paychecks through a bonus-paying plan anyway; some in fact doubled their paychecks though incentives. Not surprisingly, very few of the workers on the incentive system cared to swap their proven moneymaking programs for the experimental LRSP. Getting rid of those expensive incentive programs figured high on management's priority list in backing the LRSP. So Kaiser Steel gave incentive workers the opportunity to give up their incentive plans for participating in the LRSP, enticing them with a buyout offer of up to 5,200 hours of incentive pay, but the company got few takers. For now, Kaiser management would let the existing incentive-paid workers keep their plans, in hopes that incentive jobs would die a slow but eventual death, but the incentive issue would remain.

The committee needed to continue to meet regularly to make adjustments to the base costs and other factors that would determine the amount of fruits to be distributed in the Sharing Plan. To accomplish this, the committee created three levels of action: a "long-range committee" comprising high-level union, company and public officials (McDonald, Kaiser, Dunlop, etc.), a subcommittee of lower-ranking union and company officials, and a plant-level committee of representatives from the company and the two steelworker Locals in Fontana, 2869 and 3677. Creating the Long-Range Sharing Plan itself was complicated and time-intensive enough, but administration over time, the back-and-forth of implementing new ideas, measuring costs and determining savings and just the communication between groups and layers of groups all promised to make the initial creation of the plan the easy part of the entire undertaking.

Before the LRSP became instituted, Kaiser steelworkers had to approve the plan. Because the committee had been so tight-lipped throughout the process, 5,200 of KSC's hourly employees attended special Sharing Plan workshops in Fontana to familiarize themselves with its details before voting.

ployees Accept Long Range Sharing Plan by Three-to-One Margin at Polls

☆ ☆ ☆

5,200 Attend Workshop Sessions Before Voting

FONTANA — A strong majority of steel plant employees voted January 11 to accept a Long Range Sharing Plan regarded by many experts as one of the most forward steps taken in labor-management relations in the past two decades. Of 5,349 qualified voters going to the polls, 3,966 voted "YES" in a three-to-one decision in favor of a plan designed to do away with contract deadlines on wages and economic benefits and designed to give employees protection against loss of employment or income because of automation.

Workshops

Voting climaxed night and day workshop and question and answer sessions on the plan that were attended by over 5,200 members. This included some 800 who attended special sessions for crane operators, assigned maintenance, Tin Mill, Open Hearth, and other groups. Explanations of the plan were given by union technicians, headed by Marvin J. Miller, special assistant to David J. McDonald, president of the Steelworkers. Miller is also a member of the nine-man Long Range Committee that recommended the plan.

Vote Gratifying

Edgar F. Kaiser and David J. McDonald both expressed gratification on results of the vote, pointing out the opportunities that were opened by the plan for employees, the company and the public.

Kaiser said: "The affirmative vote evidenced that the employees of Fontana believe the new plan has merit. We are convinced that the plan offers great opportunity to the employees at the Fontana

Plant, the public and the Company.

Sound Principles

"The principles of the new plan are sound. Undoubtedly, in operating under the plan there may develop problem areas. This is usually true with any new plan. We are confident however that working together we can resolve these problem areas should they occur. We look forward to the benefits that this plan offers all the participants, including the public."

McDonald said: "We believe that our membership at the Kaiser Steel Corporation plant at Fontana has demonstrated good judgment in ratifying a plan designed solely for their future well being through its provisions of sharing of economic gains and job protection against the ever increasing impact of automation.

Bold in Concept

"This is a new idea bold in its concept and potentially far reaching in its consequences. We are supremely confident that this plan will stand the test of time.

"We are proud, as I am sure that the Kaiser workers will be, that we have joined the development of a new idea which conceivably can open the way to

(Continued on Page 3)

The clear Long-Range Sharing Plan vote outcome by Kaiser Steel workers is trumpeted in the *Ingot*.

Union and company representatives held fourteen briefing sessions, each lasting over three hours, outlining the plan and answering questions. With both the union and the company firmly behind the plan, its chances of success were high. In that election, Kaiser Steel workers approved accepting the Long-Range Sharing Plan by a conclusive three-to-one margin. An interesting difference emerges by looking inside that three-to-one figure. Production and maintenance workers of 2869 approved the plan by about a two-to-one ratio, but KSC's clerical workers of 3677 supported it by a lopsided ten to one. Internal differences aside, the election outcome meant that the LRSP had broad support plant-wide, and to give the plan some stability, the agreement would cover the Fontana plant for four years.

Some of the plan's more public figures gathered their share of accolades for their part in the experiment. Monsignor George Higgins, writing in the Chicago-based Catholic newspaper the *New World* and reprinted in KSC's *Ingot*, called "the Kaisers, father and son, the composite 'Man of the Year' for 1959." So exciting was the LRSP that Edgar Kaiser even traveled to Washington, D.C., to brief President John F. Kennedy at the White House. Edgar's hopes that the LRSP would cap rising steel prices had piqued JFK's interest as he struggled to keep the nation's inflation rate in check. A few years later, the favorable press and optimistic predictions for the Long-Range Sharing Plan continued to reflect well on Edgar: in 1966, the California Museum of Science and Industry named him "California Industrialist of the Year," citing among other things "his innovative stewardship of Kaiser Industries Corporation in achieving historic breakthroughs in industrial growth and labor relations," and calling the Fontana steel plant "one of the best-built and best-managed in the nation." And that same year, President Lyndon Johnson appointed Edgar to his nine-person Presidential Advisory Committee on Labor-Management Policy. The plan boosted the visibility of the men involved and the steel plant.

"Man I got it made!" shouted Kaiser Steel machinist D.D. Frazee after picking up his first paycheck with the Sharing Plan bonus attached. "I figured I'd get something like $20." Following the implementation of the plan, thousands of KSC employees registered this same kind of surprised and excited support. Newspapers and magazines from across the nation, many well-known publications such as the *Wall Street Journal*, *Chicago Tribune*, *Denver News*, *Los Angeles Times*, *Washington Daily News*, *Honolulu Star-Bulletin* and others covered the plan and worker reactions. The company reported saving $962,000 in March 1963, of which it distributed $312,000 to 3,390 eligible employees. The average bonus payment came to $92 per worker, so the plan's first checks received positive reviews.

Workers felt a connection to the savings Kaiser Steel used to fund the Sharing Plan's first payment check. Crane crews used to discard three-hundred-foot-length cables when they snapped but now used the severed segments elsewhere, saving the company fifty dollars per fifty-foot length. Around the plant, workers painted the prices of pieces of machinery to encourage others to treat the equipment with care. A crew of electricians developed a new universal conduit hanger that accommodated a wide range of conduit sizes. Workers won awards, such as new televisions, for the best cost-savings ideas and had their pictures featured in the *Ingot*.

Not convinced that employees picking up nails off the floor and other minor contributions could possibly add up to the $5.6 million savings that KSC reported in the plan's first six months, *Business Week* magazine suggested that other things outside worker control actually funded the LRSP's early success. After looking at KSC's performance more carefully, writers for the publication concluded, "Much, perhaps most [of the reported savings], stems from more efficient machinery, lower cost of raw materials such as ferromanganese and scrap iron, and figure-juggling that tries to account for changes in wholesale steel prices and cost-of-living tallies since 1961." But if management wanted workers to accept the Long-Range Sharing Plan, to more easily accept jobs lost to technology and liquidated in the name of cost cutting, it had to encourage workers to save money everywhere, to make them feel they had a stake in the larger picture of company success.

Incentive workers were by and large unswayed by the early results of the LRSP. Incentives had been in place at Fontana since management and the USWA signed the first labor contract, and they were in place at steel plants across America. In such incentive arrangements, the company paid a bonus to a worker (or a team of workers) who produced more than a predetermined amount or rate. Not all jobs received or were considered for receiving incentive pay; they tended to be found more often in the "finishing end" of the plant, with what was produced being closer to the consumer. Those jobs where workers themselves exercised greater control over quality and production rate than in other positions around the plant tended to have incentives. These skilled workers also enjoyed an unusual amount of freedom from constant supervision, left alone to do their work the best they could. One labor writer noted that incentive jobs like those at Kaiser were common "in steel, where much of the work is still an art, [because] output incentives focus attention on results and eliminate or minimize the supervisory task of watching all of the activities of workers." Other jobs, like welder, secretary or electrician, defied being put into an incentive program because of the nature of the work. What would targets be, and how would performance be measured, without a convenient and meaningful rubric to use, such as feet per hour or tons per hour produced? Not all incentive jobs carried the same rate of bonus; some jobs paid more than others. A committee of workers and management at contract negotiation time reviewed new jobs to be considered for incentive and determined the rate of incentive bonus, the production targets and so forth. Tom Rabone, a five-stand roller in the tin mill, pointed out that perhaps labor should not have favored incentives because all incentives "cannibalized" jobs by having fewer people do more work, and they encouraged people to work very, very hard. But they proved to be highly popular with Kaiser workers nonetheless, and the incentive committee was always considering new jobs to be given incentive pay. And since these coveted positions in the mill paid the biggest wages of any hourly jobs at the Fontana plant, these workers were naturally skeptical that the Long-Range Sharing Plan could possibly improve their situation. Rabone, a man very fond of his incentive plan, remembered, "The Long-Range Sharing Plan to me in 1959 was a threat." The percentage of workers participating in the Kaiser incentive plan dropped slowly over the next few years, but management could not eliminate the program entirely.

On the other side of the issue, those workers who voiced the most outspoken support for the Sharing Plan were workers who either had low-paying incentive jobs or, even more likely, had jobs that would never be considered for incentive pay. These steelworkers had nothing to lose by accepting the LRSP and everything to gain. The largest single group of workers in favor of trying the plan at Kaiser Steel was the plant's clerical and technical workers. The relative strength of support for the LRSP in the clerical and technical workers' local can be measured in the one-sidedness of the 1963 plan election. Expressed another way than earlier, in that vote, Local 2869 members (which included all the incentive workers at Kaiser Steel) voted 3,620 to 1,348 in favor of adopting the plan, an impressive 72.8 percent in support. By contrast, the members of Local 3677, men and women whose jobs would never have incentive plans, voted 346 to 35 in favor of the plan—an even more impressive 91 percent in support. Designers of the plan hoped that the initial support would buy the committee time to work out the bugs in the plan and weather the problems.

Initial support for the plan soon flagged, though, and grumbling about the plan became common among KSC production workers by late 1963. Many workers expressed great frustration at the shrinking amounts of LRSP bonus payments. After an initial windfall to workers, workers saw the about ninety-dollar bonuses in their October 1963 paychecks skid to just fourteen dollars by May 1964. One worker, Tony Ibarra, told the *Wall Street Journal* in June 1964 that if this trend continued, "next month we may owe the company." USWA Local 2869 leadership still largely supported the LRSP but was having increasing difficulty selling the plan to its members and explaining to them where all the fruits of the company's success had gone. For example, the company greatly improved Eagle Mountain's efficiency by adding a beneficiation plant at the mine in 1963, which upgraded the iron content of ore to 57 to 60 percent, then added a pelletizing plant, which bumped up the iron content of ore to 65 percent and formed the ore into uniform-sized balls about one-half inch in diameter, which boosted blast furnace efficiency. These improvements had a dramatic effect on operating costs at the Fontana plant, but since the LRSP left costs for iron ore from Eagle Mountain out of the computation of savings eligible for LRSP payments, the company did not feel obliged to share these particular fruits with workers.

In late 1963, when the first objections started to be heard from Kaiser workers, Sharing Plan supporters could still reasonably argue that the LRSP was still in its "shakedown period," when understandable problems would arise and adjustments would be made. While the number of objections rose, as did the tenor of those objections, the kinds of complaints raised by KSC workers did not really change. Functionally, Kaiser Steel had actually added an unfortunate "two-tiered pay system" with the advent of the Long-Range Sharing Plan, with a group of generally older and established workers earning some tremendous wages and incentive bonuses and a larger group of usually less skilled, often younger workers having an unpredictable, although never really lucrative, LRSP. The two groups came to fear and resent each other. Problems with incentive aside, a growing number of Kaiser Steel workers clamored for their jobs to be given incentive pay, much to the disappointment and displeasure of the Oakland office.

Predictably, arguments over the merits of the LRSP soon spilled over into union politics. In the 1964 election to choose Local 2869's president, one candidate, Ronnie Bitonti, challenged the sitting (pro-LRSP) president Jim Vezie, specifically in "protest against the plan." In his campaign, Vezie articulated support for the basic plan, arguing that its recent shortfalls meant that it only needed adjustment. Fallout from the controversial plan even extended its influence to national union politics. David McDonald had forged a strong connection between himself and the Long-Range Sharing Plan from its very inception, and he remained an outspoken proponent as it struggled to take off and gain acceptance. So when workers at Kaiser Steel became less supportive of the LRSP, they also became less supportive of Mr. McDonald.

Stained by his association with the increasingly unpopular Long-Range Sharing Plan, discredited by being connected to some unsavory figures in the union hierarchy and undermined by his inability to relate effectively with workers, David McDonald lost the 1965 election held at Fontana, as he did nationwide. Among Local 2869 workers, some 25 percent of whom still worked with incentive plans, a three-to-two margin supported the candidacy of I.W. Abel. Local 2869 member Steve Lakich reflected, "The sharing plan is why, I think, he [McDonald] lost the local!" Not surprisingly, though, McDonald still carried the office workers in Local 3677.

As the years passed, the Sharing Plan became more and more of a divisive issue at Fontana. In fact, the plan not only failed to remove economic issues

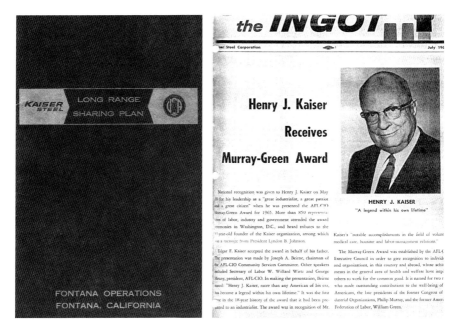

Left: An LRSP pamphlet, 1965.

Right: Henry Kaiser won a number of labor relations awards over the years, such as this one in 1965.

from the bargaining table, as Edgar Kaiser had hoped, but it also provided for a whole new kind of economic issue over which labor and management could argue. Even though the bonuses did inch up after 1964, they did so just enough to keep a semblance of popular support for the plan. Kaiser management gambled heavily in the 1959 strike settlement that their new labor relations approach would allow Kaiser Steel to leave labor problems behind and enter into a new era of prosperity while changing the course of labor relations in America. But the tidal wave that Kaiser management, and even more so David McDonald, wanted to create in with the LRSP didn't amount to much more than a ripple, and a modest one at that; no other steel plant instituted a KSC-like sharing plan. Unfortunately, the LRSP only put an added, unneeded and onerous burden on the West Coast's only mine-to-metal steel plant as it entered its third decade of operation.

Chapter 6

KAISER STEEL
AT MIDDLE AGE

Fortress Kaiser

With company profits never having reached more than uninspired levels, KSC Oakland officials hoped to jump-start the regional steel market by announcing a unilateral price cut in October 1962. Management believed that the price reduction of about twelve dollars per ton would stimulate steel-consuming industries in its service region. Anticipated productivity gains realized from increased steel sales, driven by the lower steel prices, would dovetail with the savings realized by the LRSP in a potent one-two-three economic punch and breathe new life into the Fontana operation. Happily, the strategy seemed to create the desired results for KSC's sales and profit levels, both of which increased in 1962. This launched the company down a new road of sustained profitability, with Kaiser Steel earning an aggregate $156.4 million from 1960 to 1969. The West's population growth and steel usage continued unabated, fueling this trend. For example, the seven states in KSC's primary market doubled their populations between 1940 and 1960, about twice the national growth average. Similarly, steel usage in Kaiser Steel's service area doubled in that timespan, also having about twice the growth seen nationally.

With this economic turnaround registered, the KSC boardroom had confidence to move forward more aggressively, so in August 1964, the company announced a $119 million expansion for the Fontana plant and its mines. This expansion led to KSC building its first galvanized mill.

Left: By the opening of the 1960s, Edgar Kaiser had risen to lead the business empire previously overseen by his father.

Below: An image of the Fontana steel facility looking east, with the San Gabriel Mountains in the background, circa mid-1960s.

Henry Kaiser retired from leadership of his enterprises in the late 1950s, but his companies gave his 1967 passing considerable attention.

Kaiser plowed money into both the "primary end" of the plant (which made metal) and the "finishing end" (the rolling mills that made it ready for the consumer). Kaiser Steel had placed itself ahead of the industry curve by adding a cutting-edge oxygen shop in 1958, but staying on technological top was a constantly moving target. While continuous casting had been in use and much discussed for decades, steel casting was still new technology, and violent "breakouts" with molten steel spilling out of the machinery were common, so Kaiser management rejected adding a caster in the mid-1960s.

A real challenge on the horizon in the 1960s for Kaiser and indeed all U.S. steel producers was the increasing penetration of foreign steel into the US market. The 1959 strike introduced many steel-starved American buyers to the foreign product when domestic makers could not deliver. The overseas plants were generally newer than most American plants, used more new technology and benefited from the rash of newly found ore sources—in Australia, for instance—all of which allowed plants in a handful of developing countries to compete successfully. Unfortunately for Kaiser, the western steel market became the most inundated with foreign steel.

KSC leadership did not ignore this influx of foreign steel. The 1965 annual report claimed, "Your Company is studying every possible way of coping with this competition." Kaiser's second generation of leadership began looking across the Pacific Ocean for markets. While expensive American finished steel products would not likely find many buyers in Asia, Kaiser Steel could still competitively sell (less value-added) raw materials to Asian steelmakers. In 1961, Kaiser Steel Corporation signed a ten-year deal with Mitsubishi of Japan to sell the industrial giant ten million tons of iron ore from Eagle Mountain. The slightly processed ore would be prepared as if it was bound for Fontana but would just continue its train ride to Long Beach and be loaded onto ships. Shipments to Kaiser Steel's competitors across the Pacific continued through the early 1970s. In 1962, Kaiser Steel entered into an agreement with the Australian firm Conzinc Riotinto to develop and share control of a massive iron ore reserve in Western Australia, the Hamersley Mine. Kaiser owned a 40 percent stake

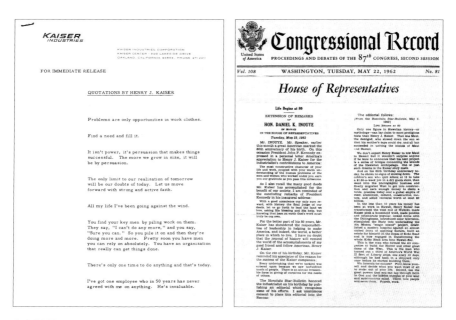

Left: HJK's passing was another opportunity to share his quotes, such as in this press release.

Right: Henry Kaiser spent his last decade in Hawaii developing areas around Honolulu, so a Hawaiian congressman honored Kaiser on his eightieth birthday.

in Hamersley Holdings Ltd., which sold hundreds of millions of dollars of iron ore to Japanese firms. Geologists estimated that the site contained billions of tons of high-grade (50–68 percent iron) ore, making it far larger than Eagle Mountain. By 1964, contracts to Japanese steel mills totaled over half a million dollars, with more to follow in later years. Lastly, in 1967, KSC acquired more coal fields in British Columbia, Canada. KSC pumped tens of millions of dollars into developing the Canadian site into a state-of-the-art coal mine, complete with a railroad spur and a ship-loading facility. Like with the Hamersley product, the British Columbian coal could be sold to any company, but the fine coking properties of the ore meant that it would be especially attractive to steelmakers. Consequently, in 1967, KSC announced that it had just closed a deal to sell forty million tons of coal to a Japanese steelmaker. Shipments began in 1969. These projects became solid moneymakers for the company, but one wonders about the wisdom of strengthening the competition like this. With the company selling so much raw material internationally, management decided that it might as well try to make money from transporting the ore, too. Therefore, in 1968, Kaiser

Finally, the plan provides distribution of the employees' net
re in the gains on a monthly basis. The plan thus offers em-
yees potential new sources of income by sharing savings as
y occur during the actual course of production. It also per-
s the parties to agree on the use of a portion of the gains
duced by the plan for making improvements or adding to
urance, retirement, vacation, holiday and other benefits not
vided generally in the industry. The remaining net gains
l be distributed in pay checks directly to the employee: ach
nth as an addition to their regular pay.

The plan provides that, even after the Sharing Plan is in-
lled, incentive coverage will continue for employees now
rking on incentive. Employees not now covered by incentives
bout 60% of total employment) will participate in cost
ings, in addition to their regular pay, through the receipt
payments under the Long Range Sharing Plan.

Sharing by Incentive Employees

loyees now on incentives may transfer to the Long Range
aring Plan in a variety of ways.

(1) The employees on any incentive plan may decide, by
majority vote, to cancel the existing incentive and transfer to the Long Range Sharing Plan.

(2) When the company so offers, the employees on an in-

DECEMBER 13, 1962 — Edgar F. Kaiser reported to The President the possibility that the Long Range Committee would arrive at agreement and finalize the Sharing Plan that weekend.
Here he is shown at the White House where he talked over the

After the 1959 strike, Edgar became the second family member recognized as a business
and labor leader. Here, Edgar speaks with President John F. Kennedy.

Steel joined forces with Kaiser Aluminum to create United International Shipping Corporation.

Another element of the Kaiser response to cheap foreign steel was to "take them to court." An early example came in the 1962 annual report, in which KSC announced that "the Company submitted data to the U.S. Commissioner of Customs charging that hot rolled carbon steel sheet is being sold in the United States by Japanese steel companies at prices lower than Japanese home market prices." Legislation preventing dumping—i.e., selling foreign-made products in the United States for below the cost of production or less than in home markets—had existed for decades, and Kaiser Steel management wanted it invoked. As it turned out, actually proving dumping and then getting changes implemented in trade was harder than it sounded, and domestic steelmakers like Kaiser achieved little success in slowing foreign steel sales. A 1966 article in the *Ingot* described this relentless assault on KSC's home turf from foreign steel mills leading to the company becoming "Fortress Kaiser."

MORE LABOR TROUBLE AT FONTANA

Henry J.'s flexibility in dealing with labor would have been put to the test with the changing face of labor relations in the 1960s. The Fontana workforce

grew over the decades: from a few hundred in 1942, it reached 7,344 in 1955 and peaked at 9,357 in 1967. Kaiser Steel employment in the late 1960s totaled several thousand more if the mines, fabricating yards and sales offices were included. And importantly, the types of persons who worked at Kaiser changed. While exact numbers breaking down KSC's workforce into racial and gender categories over the years are no longer available, it is clear from interviews with retirees and examining photographs that the vast majority of production workers at Fontana remained white men. That percentage began to change ever so slightly in the 1960s. And while the percentage of steelworkers coming from groups historically excluded from this work changed, demands increased for greater opportunities for all people at the plant. The most vocal group demanding that the company and the union change their attitude in hiring and promotion practices at Fontana were women.

The steel industry remained unusually intransigent to breaking down the unwritten but still real exclusion of women from production jobs through the twentieth century. At Kaiser Steel, neither the male-dominated management nor the male-dominated union stepped forward to hire women in production jobs, and complaints by women that they should have more job opportunities and receive equal treatment on the shop floor fell on deaf ears through the 1950s. The big "break" for women to obtain a small number of production jobs at Fontana came when KSC opened its tin mill in 1952, as discussed earlier. There remains no written evidence that female steelworkers at Fontana challenged this state of affairs in any numbers in the 1950s.

A few women at the Fontana plant spoke up in favor of change. Minnie Luksich, a tin mill worker and USWA grievance woman, became a chief instigator of Fontana women who challenged the gender status quo after she attended union-sponsored civil rights workshops in the early 1960s. The union wanted to make their grievance people more aware of and sensitive to the issues of racial discrimination in steel plants, although it appears to have had no interest in gender issues. Luksich remembered, "I would go to these meetings and absorb things." KSC's women knew that there were a large number of jobs around the plant that laid-off workers could perform. Getting a woman on the contract negotiating team (which the president of the union local assembled) would have been greatly appreciated, too. Even though the union ostensibly represented all its members, Luksich recalled that she "would go [to union meetings] with several of the girls. It was obvious that they [union officials] were trying to smooth things over, you know, and it was obvious that they weren't as sincere in their efforts as I was....I had no help from any of the union officials, they just thought I was a trouble maker."

By 1968, a potent year for protest across America, dozens of Kaiser Steel's female employees had reached their breaking point with their employer and, to an extent, their union. After being shut out from the best-paying jobs with the company and the most influential positions within the union (except for Local 3677's president FitzGerald) and ignored at meetings and negotiations, Kaiser's female steelworkers went public with their frustration. Dozens of female tin mill workers launched a march, complete with large placard signs and loud chants, outside the contract negotiations being held in Fontana in September 1968, complaining that they faced job discrimination. They were not arguing that tin flippers be recognized (and paid) for the skill they had; instead, they simply demanded that they be treated like card-carrying steelworkers, not as second-class "female steelworkers." At that time, about seventy women in the tin mill were on layoff because the company did not have enough work. Through increased use of automation in the tin mill and changing demands in the tin market, there was less need for flippers. If a male steelworker found himself on layoff status, he could be reassigned to another production job around the plant, but that was not the case with a woman. What infuriated these women was that Kaiser could have placed these seventy women someplace, had them do something around the plant, but the company chose not to. In 1968, the company reported a profit of $33.9 million on sales of $426.9 million, with the prospect of 1969 being roughly similar—good numbers for KSC. In fact, business was good enough that the company had started a program to hire 450 "long-term unemployed" men from the area, many of color. This decision infuriated KSC's women all the more. The signs they carried in the march sported messages such as "Kaiser Hires 400 Hard Core, Women Laid Off?" "Kaiser Is Discriminating" and "Jobs for the Minority—Women!" A determined Minnie Luksich told a local newspaper reporter, "We don't want the new contract signed until our women have their jobs back." The protest briefly grabbed a bit of local media attention, but it did not sway the negotiators.

Tension arising from the Long-Range Sharing Plan, a growing backlog of unprocessed grievances and the demands of angry women formed the backdrop for the 1972 contract negotiations. In fact, tensions rose to such a pitch that Fontana suffered from a six-week strike sanctioned by the USWA leadership in Pittsburgh. Unlike the 1959 strike, though, Kaiser steelworkers did not follow the industry out in a nationwide strike but instead hit the picket lines strictly over local issues. Ironically, the very thing that was supposed to smooth out Fontana's labor problems, the Long-Range Sharing Plan, instead had brought tensions to a head and actually precipitated a stoppage.

The Long-Range Sharing Plan was designed to be "interactive," an ongoing, dynamic work in progress that workers and management constantly tinkered with as conditions and demands changed. The plan was continually updated, and then the newest plan, or several versions of the plan, were agreed to by the LRSP Committee and presented to workers for their approval through a general vote. But as frustrations of workers mounted that the LRSP was not all its proponents had promised, opposition to it among the rank and file grew. With the steel company doing well in 1963, when the plan first emerged, and with the impressive initial savings first realized, early payments to participating workers at KSC ran high and had averaged about 19 percent of take-home pay since 1963. But with savings quickly increasingly harder to come by, the plan failed to produce substantial returns to workers by the second half of the 1960s; in some months, Sharing Plan bonus checks came to zero. Usually, the terms and goals for the Long-Range Sharing Plan were negotiated by teams who sat on the LRSP Committee, who then passed the plan along to workers, who either accepted or rejected it. In 1972, the LRSP Committee could not come to an agreement that all parties approved. In fact, in that year, Local 2869 committee members rejected the company's plan. Convinced that most workers would accept the company's latest version of the plan, management went ahead and offered it to workers for a vote anyway.

In February 1972, members of USWA Local 2869 narrowly rejected the latest version of the Long-Range Sharing Plan favored by the company by a vote of 2,446 to 2,179. Local 2869's leadership, which was against the LRSP, wanted the company to increase the number of workers eligible for incentive pay—which would, of course, directly work against the company's ultimate plan. Kaiser Steel employees enjoyed an attractive pay and benefits package; that was not at issue in 1972. In fact, just three months before the Sharing Plan vote, Local 2869 members voted to ratify a new general labor contract, which provided for a generous 15 percent increase to wages. Sadly, the Long-Range Sharing Plan had sowed deep fissures within the Fontana workforce. Fighting over the plan divided the membership of 2869 and pitted Fontana's two locals of the United Steelworkers of America against each other. While production and maintenance workers in Local 2869 narrowly voted down the company's latest version of the LRSP, clerical and technical workers in Local 3677 voted by an overwhelming majority to accept it. The much smaller 3677 reported that 318 members voted to accept and 29 voted to reject, nearly a ten-to-one margin. In past LRSP elections, the results of the two locals had been combined, delivering the labor vote as a single voice for all wage workers at Kaiser Steel. But in this election, leadership of the larger local ignored the votes of the smaller one. This was no mere procedural detail, either. If the votes of the two locals had been combined, as they had been in years past, the cumulative vote total would have rendered the opposite outcome: a narrow victory for accepting the company's version of the Long-Range Sharing Plan and thus no strike. Local 2869 president Dino Papavero told local newspaper reporters that he knew of no rule that mandated the votes of the two locals be combined. Papavero flippantly noted, "In 1968, for instance, they had 2,800 for approval and 1,800 against, so it made no difference whether it was included or not. Now this is a completely different thing." A critic of the Sharing Plan, Papavero used his high office to stage a coup of sorts in overturning the vote of a majority of KSC workers. Giving Papavero cover was USWA District 38 director McGee, who approved the split vote. The provocative move by President Papavero guaranteed a fight. *Steel Labor* acknowledged the difference in opinion between the two locals, noting, "The production and maintenance local union asked for and received authorization to strike while the office and technical local union was content to go along with the plan." The national office of the USWA tread carefully in this interunion squabble. The USWA provided monetary strike relief for members, but those funds did not become available for three weeks, putting Local 2869 workers in a real economic squeeze.

This latest stoppage brought widespread finger-pointing and dissent among workers. The clerical and technical workers had selected a woman to head their local, Marty FitzSimmons, a rare female local president at the time, and she refused to have her members take a backseat to Papavero's. Incensed by Papavero's action, FitzSimmons threatened to seek a court injunction to end the strike. She told reporters that because of Papavero's action, "we have obtained legal counsel." This tension manifested itself in a very tangible and concrete way: the picket line. USWA Local 2869 received approval from the USWA headquarters for its strike, and it manned a picket line at the plant's gates. On the other hand, Kaiser's clerical and technical workers still had a working labor contract, but in order to report to work, they had to cross 2869's picket line. Members of Kaiser's clerical and technical union local had been granted safe passage through the picket line by special arrangement between the two local officers, but apparently that deal had not fully filtered down to Fontana's plant gates. FitzSimmons issued a warning to her membership: "We're advising our members not to go to their local for a pass [to enter the plant through the gates] because we don't feel that it is safe." While the two locals scrapped with each other, regional

Local media reporting on women striking at Kaiser Steel, 1972.

and national levels of the United Steelworkers tried to minimize the family feud. USWA District 38 regional director Frank McGee chastised the area members: "Union people should not be fighting other union people. I feel like I'm trapped in the middle of a shooting match between Production-Maintenance and Clerical-Technical." United Steelworkers president I.W. Abel asserted his "full support" for the strike and, at least in the local press, did not mention the split between the two locals.

Amid the disintegration of any semblance of labor harmony at Fontana during the strike, rumors began to circulate among workers and the press that company leaders had endured enough headaches at the plant and were seriously considering taking some drastic actions. According to the gossip, the company's persistent less-than-stunning profit levels, compounded with more recent labor problems, had motivated KSC management in Oakland to cut its losses and either abandon or curtail steelmaking. Kaiser Steel retiree Abe Rothstein vividly remembered that while on picket duty during the strike, a colleague predicted, "Within five years that open hearth is going to be shut down. Kaiser's going to be running the finishing mills. They're going to be importing slabs and just rolling them"; the move would save the company considerable money and headache, plus "teach the Steelworkers a lesson." The stories became so widespread that management was asked to respond to them. Addressing the scuttlebutt in a local newspaper about two weeks into the strike, a Kaiser Steel spokesperson said, "We can't say this will never happen, but in the context of this strike, no, a steel mill is not that easily portable"—hardly a commitment for continued steelmaking. Indeed, the year preceding the strike gave workers, managers and stockholders little to smile about. According to the 1971 KSC annual report, the firm earned a meager $355,000 in profits, added $36.6 million in long-term debt, witnessed imports grabbing a record 30 percent of the western steel market and endured "sharply increased costs for labor, supplies, and services." Mark Anthony, who became Kaiser Steel president in 1975, insisted twenty years later, "I was working for a company that wanted to stay in the steel business."

After Kaiser workers had been out on strike for about five weeks, on March 10, labor and

Women sue Kaiser for job rights

By FLOYD RINEHART
Sun-Telegram Staff Writer

FONTANA — Sixteen women employed at the Kaiser Steel Corp. tin mill here have filed charges of job discrimination against the firm and their union, United Steelworkers of America (USWA), Local 2869.

The charges were filed with the Equal Employment Opportunity Commission in Los Angeles by Fontella Yarbrough and 15 other women workers: Pauline Raska, Helen Verlich, Pearl Hill, Helen Harrison, Ann Averett, Hazel Allen, Agned Welty, Helen Novak, Vivian Kaiser, Lyle Hoon, Lois Holloway, Cleda Craven, Louise Curtis, Frances Amicucci and Rolly Petric.

They accuse Kaiser and Local 2869 of:
1. Maintaining segregated job classifications, lines of progression and opportunities on the basis of sex which denies promotions to women.
2. Hiring men for jobs that women can perform, while women are on lay-off.
3. Requiring employes to work at certain labor jobs that generally are too difficult for women and deny women access to promotion lines because they have not performed these labor jobs.
4. Excluding women in the shear and electrolytic lines from participating in incentive plans, while men in the units have received substantial incentive earnings.
5. Denying women the right to

(Continued on B—5, Column 1)

SAN BERNARDINO

Local media reporting on KSC female tin mill workers suing the company in 1973 for denying female employees equal access to jobs.

management began "round the clock" negotiations. On March 15, workers voted on a plan supported by members of the LRSP Committee. No doubt responding to the severe hardship the strike had caused them, KSC workers voted to end the strike and accept the new compensation plan, with 84 percent of those voting in favor of the revised plan. But only about half of those employees eligible even bothered to cast their vote.

But why did half of Kaiser workers shun the March 15 vote? Perhaps the answer can be found in the compromise solution workers voted on. The approved package allowed those KSC workers on the incentive plan to keep it, while all employees could choose to join one of three slightly different Long-Range Sharing Plans. The same ballot also moved the expiration date of the Sharing Plan to coincide with that of the general labor contract. While the vote ended the strike and opened the plant, it did not solve the underlying problems behind the strike: management's desire to end the incentive pay system and go to 100 percent LRSP participation and the inability of the LRSP to make workers feel that they were receiving fair compensation from the company. By the 1970s, the old company motto of "Together We Build" seemed pretty hollow. In the 1940s, Kaiser Steel execs looked at labor relations as a part of the business where KSC had an edge over the eastern competition. But by the early 1970s, Kaiser Steel execs looked at labor relations as a part of the business that was a drain to the company.

Fontana Hunkers Down After the 1972 Strike

In 1973, Kaiser Steel's superintendent of industrial relations, Richard W. Welch, issued a white paper that reviewed the changing face of labor relations at KSC. Welch acknowledged the sagging morale at Fontana, among Kaiser Steel workers and managers alike, writing, "It has been said that 'Kaiser isn't Kaiser anymore.'" He gently agreed with that assessment and even suggested that much of this unfortunate change in perceived labor harmony was seen in a general decline in flexibility in dealing with problems, good-faith bargaining, openness and respect of all the parties involved. When Welch broached the topic of salvaging a healthy dialogue between labor and management, the steel plant was still smarting from the forty-four-day strike the year before. The number of employee-generated complaints about conditions and management stood at 380, a surprising number for a small plant. Welch called on labor relations at KSC to rediscover the "historical policies" of the company, embodied in the motto "Together We Build." Clearly, the inability of Kaiser's employees and managers to work smoothly and effectively together was not in keeping with the spirit of Henry J. Kaiser and was threatening the company's success.

Company hiring strategies in the 1960s and 1970s perhaps exacerbated employee dissatisfaction. KSC had always depended on a small but critical infusion of talent from outside the immediate Fontana area to fill certain needs. That trend notwithstanding, KSC made a large number of high-profile appointments in the 1970s that left the impression that a new breed of "industry men" had assumed control over the company, and these new men might be responsible for the feeling that "Kaiser isn't Kaiser anymore." In 1976, James Will replaced M.J. Smith (who had held his position since 1969) as works manager. Whereas the top executives of Kaiser Steel

KAISER STEEL OF FONTANA

maintained offices in Oakland, the works manager had his office in Fontana and was the highest-ranking company official on-site. KSC did not hire in-house to replace Smith; after stints at U.S. Steel and Miami Industries in the Midwest, Will came west in 1974, when Kaiser hired him as general superintendent at Fontana, a position he held until his 1976 promotion. Will was no steelworker; he received an MBA from Duquesne University. Kaiser Steel quickly followed up on Will's appointment with that of Robert Stanier as superintendent of Fontana's rolling mills a month later. Stanier had similar credentials as Will: an MBA (University of Chicago) and years of experience at U.S. Steel (at Gary, Indiana). And there were many others. Mark Anthony admitted that this eastern managerial influx changed the atmosphere in labor relations, suggesting, "I think the eastern mills did not have the labor relations recorded that Kaiser had....Some of the managers came out with pretty much a hard-nosed attitude about labor." The new managers brought a wealth of experience to the Fontana operation, and to their credit, the plant did not endure another sanctioned strike after the 1972 stoppage, but they did not bring any kind of "golden age" of labor harmony to Fontana.

And the steel industry in the 1970s faced ever more challenges from expensive environmental regulation. Mirroring the greater public demand for pollution control, in the 1960s, the federal government assumed a far more aggressive role. The Clean Air Act of 1963, Motor Vehicle Air Pollution Control Act of 1964 and Air Quality Act of 1967 ratcheted up Washington's direct involvement in regulating sources of air pollution, with California, specifically Southern California, in the vanguard. It was in this surge of regulatory activity that the powerful Environmental Protection Agency (EPA) was born. Stationary polluters nationwide, such as steel plants, had to meet increasingly stringent laws. In Kaiser Steel's case, that meant adhering to the toughest local standards in the nation, as it had for several decades, plus conforming to whatever the EPA dictated; it was clear that many millions of dollars would be spent on pollution control in the years ahead.

The EPA wasted little time after its establishment in singling out Kaiser Steel as a serious regional air polluter. In 1973, an inspector for the new agency judged several smokestacks at the Fontana plant to be in violation of various regulations. That judgment was bad enough, but the Kaiser plant was already out of compliance with county standards enforced by the San Bernardino Air Pollution Control District and was operating under a variance issued by that agency. The San Bernardino County Board of Supervisors had adopted a new

Air Control and Water Conservation

Starting in 1953, electrostatic precipitators have cleaned more
than 95% of the smoke emissions from the stacks of Fontana's nine open hearth furnaces.

During an experimental test, with the electrostatic precipitators turned off,
left, the oxygen steelmaking plant stacks cloud the sky; after they are switched on
during normal operation, the sky is left clear.

Throughout the decades, Kaiser Steel addressed the issue of air pollution;
this is circa 1970.

KSC used the 1972 strike, as it did in 1959, to show that the region's air quality issues existed even without contribution from KSC's steelmaking.

standard for emissions of stationary polluters the year before the EPA slapped its ruling on Kaiser Steel. The county gave Kaiser Steel until 1975 to conform to its standards. At the behest of the company, in 1973, meetings between KSC and the EPA began to address Kaiser's violations; the meetings led to a consent order issued in 1974. Kaiser Steel and the EPA agreed to a host of changes in its operations to bring it into compliance. The greatest challenge came from cleaning up the operation of the coke ovens. The EPA insisted that Kaiser engineers trap more particulates from the coke oven smokestacks and remove more sulfur from the recycled coke oven gas. Additionally, pollution control devices needed to be added to the open hearth furnaces and the BOP (basic oxygen process) shop. Lastly, the 1974 consent agreement demanded that Kaiser engineers find new ways to cut up scrap metal being "charged" into furnaces, because using cutting torches released high levels of iron oxides. Initial estimates suggested that compliance with the 1974 decree would cost KSC $20 million for implementation. Conforming to pollution standards was going to add a new level of urgency to Kaiser Steel's need to generate profits.

Observers initially released optimistic growth forecasts in America's steel market for the 1970s. One prediction called for national steel production to rise from the 1969 level of 141.3 million tons to 175 million tons by 1980. Indeed, Kaiser Steel's financial situation did perk up appreciably by the mid-1970s. Production levels hovered around 3 million tons yearly, and earnings climbed from low or nonexistent early in the decade ($335,000 in profits in 1971 and $8.8 million in losses in 1972) to back-to-back record high profits in 1973 ($52.7 million) and 1974 ($66.5 million). The 1974 annual report contained good news for stockholders: a second straight year of solid sales and profits. But management still noted that profits would have to remain as robust as they had been lately because they believed it "necessary to double our annual capital expenditure" for modernization of the Fontana operation in years ahead; staying in the steel business was getting more expensive.

With the entire industry suddenly gaining some optimism for future growth in the early 1970s, Kaiser's Oakland-based leadership decided to put the Fontana plant back on the list of America's most modern steel plants with an expansion program breathtaking in its scope and cost. KSC's Mark Anthony credits Bill Roesch, president of Kaiser Industries, with putting forth the idea. In 1975, KSC announced an audacious $213 million expansion program for its Fontana plant. The program would (finally) replace Fontana's decades-old open hearth furnaces with oxygen furnaces; 100 percent of KSC steel would be made with oxygen. Going to 100 percent oxygen would have made KSC up to date even by global standards. Kaiser management went even further. That new BOP shop would be mated to a continuous caster, a method of forming metal that was among the most important single advances in steelmaking in the twentieth century. Continuous casting bypasses the labor- and energy-intensive intermediate steps of reducing the thickness of steel from its molded form (ingots) in various mills by moving them and reheating them in soaking pits. The method gets its name from how it accepts molten steel in one end of the mill and forms a continuous feed of solidifying steel through a long, water-cooled, ski-slope-shaped caster at the other end—drawn down by gravity, bypassing the ingot step entirely and forming semi-finished steel of very high quality. Adopting the oxygen/caster system would lower

the steelmaking process

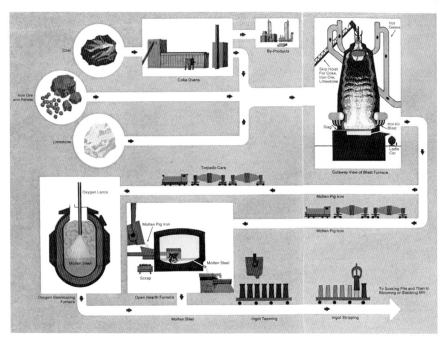

This image depicts the flow of product through the steelworks with the first BOP shop. The 1970s expansion added another oxygen furnace and a continuous caster.

costs 12 to 15 percent, and 75 percent of the money used for the upgrade would qualify for a new tax credit; the new technology made undeniable financial sense. On the other hand, adopting a continuous caster would immediately render several significant parts of the plant unnecessary, wiping out hundreds of jobs. The Oakland office began work in 1975 and planned to have the new oxygen shop and caster on line in 1978.

However, unforeseen by steel industry leaders, including Kaiser management, the bottom fell out of the world steel market in late 1975, and it entered into a steep and prolonged decline. The early 1970s steel boom went bust and plunged the worldwide steel industry into mayhem. Strong steel prices and growing steel demand had encouraged investors in many countries to build steel plants, and in those countries not having an established steel sector, investors built new, high-tech operations (i.e., oxygen and casting). This steel mill–building boom dovetailed with a sudden reversal of steel demand, led by cuts in the high-rise office building

The Fontana steelworks with the addition of BOP Shop No. 2, 1978, looking north and west; BOP Shop No. 2 is about in the middle.

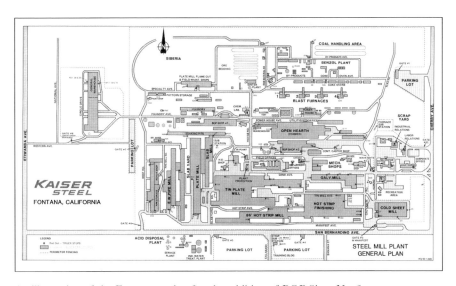

An illustration of the Fontana works after the addition of BOP Shop No. 2.

and shipbuilding industries. Sales analysis at KSC had foreseen some softening in the 1975 steel market, but according to Anthony, "Nobody expected [it] to get as bad so fast."

The 1970s global steel crisis hit the Kaiser Steel Corporation at a particularly bad time. Struggling with the price pressure from imports, dealing with spiraling utility and pollution costs, shouldering high debt going into the 1970s, then piling on the debt of the recent expansion caught managers flat-footed. Kaiser Steel posted near-record profits in 1975 of $80.5 million on strong sales of $725 million but noted in its annual report the "diminished Western steel market in the second half of the year": a downturn in the market had begun. Western steel consumption nose-dived from 11 million tons in 1974 to just 7.4 million tons in 1975. The Oakland KSC boardroom could now fully appreciate the epic crisis upon it. In 1976, profits dropped by half to $43.6 million. Then in 1977, with the effects of the steel crisis even more fully realized, KSC barely even posted a profit, reporting earnings of just $4.3 million; domestic operations incurred a $45.9 million loss. Good news was hard to find in the steelmaking portion of KSC.

With the downturn of the company's fortunes, Kaiser Steel management tried to get some breathing room on pollution standards compliance. After lengthy negotiations, in May 1977, Kaiser and these regulatory agencies agreed on a new plan to address the pollution created from Fontana's coke ovens. The company had to spend another $5 million on an "accelerated smoke control program" by the end of 1978, add another seventy-four full-time workers to combat coke oven emission specifically and spend another $10 million, or whatever was necessary, to install new equipment to more cleanly "push" the hot coke out of the ovens. Shortly thereafter, KSC agreed to pay $1 million each to the EPA and the California Air Pollution Control Fund and $100,000 to San Bernardino County to settle past disputes. Kaiser engineers could not even promise that they could find ways to meet all the regulations imposed on the plant, regardless of money. From the plant's genesis through 1978, Kaiser Steel invested approximately $138 million on pollution control measures at the Fontana plant and its supporting mines. But almost half of that amount, about $62 million, was spent just in 1977 and 1978. And those figures did not include maintenance and operating costs, which ran over $18 million in 1978 and were predicted to increase in the years ahead.

On February 9, 1979, KSC president Mark Anthony dedicated the new oxygen furnace and caster (BOP Shop No. 2), approximately one year after the scheduled opening. By that late date, the price tag had swollen to $233 million. Wanting to put the best face on a bleak situation Anthony assured the

A photo of the steel plant with BOP Shop No. 2, the tall structure in the background, 1978.

crowd assembled at the Fontana ceremony, "We're here to stay and we mean to prove it." But the expansion failed to live up to its promises. Unexpected and numerous start-up problems (for which casters are well known), more cost overruns and inability to use the equipment (or the entire plant, for that matter) at full capacity wiped out any positive impact that the new BOP shop and caster might have brought. Arguably, it was actually a much bigger furnace than Kaiser needed or ever would need, making the possibility of running at peak efficiency unlikely; the company had overbuilt. In fact, the new technology immediately became an economic black hole, sucking up the company's dwindling cash. Problems aside, the new oxygen shop produced its first heat of steel in October 1978. The new furnaces and caster produced its first heat of steel in March 1979, yielding the desired "fine-grain, high-strength" steel demanded in pipe and food can manufacture. Unfortunately, problems in the new BOP shop persisted, so management chose to reactivate two mothballed open hearths to make steel in April 1979, a move costing millions of dollars. And the caster experienced its share of problems, too. Just like in 1942, when the new Kaiser steel plant needed to import trained workers with the requisite special skills, so too in the 1970s were special skills needed to operate a continuous caster. KSC sent crews of workers to a U.S. Steel facility in Texas to watch and learn, then bring back to Fontana those skills. The aforementioned trickiness of casting meant that

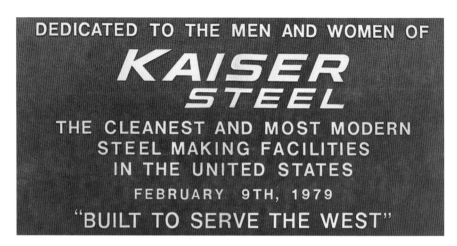

DEDICATED TO THE MEN AND WOMEN OF

KAISER
STEEL

THE CLEANEST AND MOST MODERN
STEEL MAKING FACILITIES
IN THE UNITED STATES

FEBRUARY 9TH, 1979

"BUILT TO SERVE THE WEST"

Above: This bronze plaque hung inside BOP Shop No. 2. By the 1970s, KSC's motto "Together We Build" seems to have been replaced by "Built to Serve the West."

Opposite: The highly efficient continuous caster, which accepted red-hot steel, cooling it into a long continuous solid, in Kaiser's new oxygen shop, 1978.

for a few months in 1979, 7 percent of the pours KSC workers attempted resulted in breakouts (of molten metal within the caster), causing shutdown, a bottleneck of production at the plant and a costly cleanup. By 1980, the rate of breakouts had dropped almost in half and downtime was just one-fourth of what it was in 1979, but that first year was rough. The years 1979 and 1980 only brought more losses for Kaiser Steel Corporation, which in turn led to more pink slips given to Kaiser steelworkers.

Facing an uncertain western steel market and suffering from a profound cash flow problem, Kaiser managers started unloading company assets to pay the bills. In August 1979, KSC sold its share of the Australian Hamersley mine to partner Conzinc Riotinto for $207.5 million, which net Kaiser $64.3 million. That same year, KSC sold half its shares of Kaiser Resources Ltd. In 1979, Kaiser Steel marked another first for a steel maker in the United States: it began talks with Japan's number two steelmaker Nippon Kokan Kk. (NKK) to explore their purchase of the Fontana operation, making KSC the first American integrated steel producer to consider purchase by a foreign company. The talks with NKK fell through, as did talks with domestic steelmaker LTV to buy Fontana in 1980, but the clear desire of the Oakland head office to offload the steel plant was now a matter of public record. Mark Anthony's efforts adding new equipment could not stem the flow of red ink or save his job; in January 1980, he stepped down as KSC

president, ending thirty-four years of service to Kaiser Steel. KSC was in very serious trouble.

Anthony's replacement as Kaiser Steel's president and CEO was a Kaiser family member, but the magic of the Kaiser name had lost a great deal of its luster around Fontana. Edgar, who retired at the end of 1979 because of his failing health, appointed his son Edgar Jr. as the new chief executive. Company press releases optimistically cited the younger Kaiser's tough and

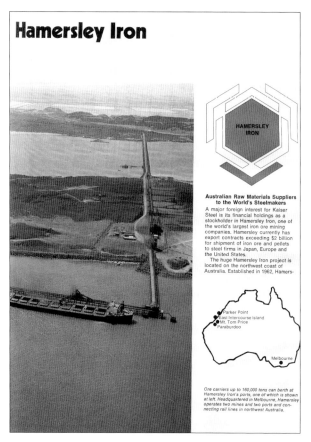

Hamersley Iron

HAMERSLEY
IRON

Australian Raw Materials Suppliers to the World's Steelmakers

A major foreign interest for Kaiser Steel is its financial holdings as a stockholder in Hamersley Iron, one of the world's largest iron ore mining companies. Hamersley currently has export contracts exceeding $2 billion for shipment of iron ore and pellets to steel firms in Japan, Europe and the United States.

The huge Hamersley Iron project is located on the northwest coast of Australia. Established in 1962, Hamers-

Parker Point
East Intercourse Island
Mt. Tom Price
Paraburdoo

Melbourne

Ore carriers up to 160,000 tons can berth at Hamersley Iron's ports, one of which is shown at left. Headquartered in Melbourne, Hamersley operates two mines and two ports and connecting rail lines in northwest Australia.

Right: Part of KSC's Australian iron operation, 1970s.

Below: A photo of a vessel that was part of KSC's shipping operation, 1970s.

successful leadership of the British Columbia coal-mining venture and other elements of the family empire. The young Kaiser exec told shareholders in the company's 1979 annual report, "Our direction in 1980 is clear. We will analyze each asset and each operation to determine its ability to stand on its own and to provide an adequate return. We will not hesitate to change the size or focus of the company if it appears that we would do better be selling or modifying an asset or operation." High labor costs, skyrocketing pollution costs, ever growing foreign competition, excess steelmaking capacity, overstaffing, surging utility costs and uneven steel demand forced immediate attention and difficult choices. Although he never said so at the time, years later, Edgar Jr. admitted that his father had sent him to Fontana to close it down. Referring to a private family meeting, Edgar Jr. told a newspaper interviewer, "We were both in tears. I knew what it meant. Nobody else saw it, but I knew what I had to do." Edgar Jr. had to cut capacity, dismember the firm and "break up a lot of steel....I had to go out after 30 percent of the work force at Fontana....It sure wasn't fun." KSC discontinued dividend payment on common stock and sold a portion of the Cushenbury limestone mine to Kaiser Cement Corporation for $3 million. Kaiser Steel unloaded the other half of its share in the British Columbia coal operation and its international shipping subsidiary. At the Fontana plant, hundreds of employees lost their jobs, both wage and salary workers. The 11 percent cut in workforce size came from consolidating managerial responsibilities and from closing the open hearth furnaces, the cold roll sheet mill, the continuous weld pipe mill and BOP Shop No. 1. Edgar Jr. left the chairmanship after a year and was replaced by Stephen A. Girard, a man with forty-plus years of managerial experience in various Kaiser empire firms. Through the *Ingot*, KSC's board reported that the sale of assets by Edgar generated money that was "reinvested in the short-term money market, [and] has produced a higher return than the previous investments would have generated," so that "Kaiser Steel now has the flexibility and liquidity to evaluate long-range plans." Girard was hardly in an enviable position.

In the midst of this uncertain and volatile situation, where KSC's day-to-day existence was in doubt, Fontana steelworkers mulled over early retirement and, if terminated, looked for other employment. Moved to save their livelihoods, a majority of USWA Local 2869 members voted in 1980 to cut into their own pay and benefits to save their jobs. Led by Local 2869 president Frank Anglin, 59 percent of the membership voted to give back a dollar an hour in future cost-of-living raises as a concession to KSC management. A vocal minority resisted; Abe Rothstein rejected the "give-back" because "right now, this is the first time in the history of the human race that a working man…has earned enough money not only to pay the rent, and keep the shoes on his kids' feet and fed, but able to go to the movies and even have a vacation." The 59 percent of Local 2869 who sided with Anglin felt like retiree John Trunoske, who remembered he was "glad to take that cut. I would have taken twice that cut." The closeness of the vote indicated the thorniness of the steelworkers' situation. The outcome of the election meant little in the end, however, as the USWA leadership in Pittsburgh blocked 2869's move, informing the Fontana local's leadership, "We take raises and benefits, we don't take cuts." In offering to take a pay and benefit cut, Kaiser steelworkers followed the lead taken by their

Edgar Kaiser Jr., the last Kaiser family member to lead Kaiser Steel, 1980.

brethren in other industrial firms across America. Around this same time, America's Big Three automakers, General Motors, Ford and Chrysler, all asked for and received "give-backs" from their workers. Kaiser Steel was part of a larger decline.

In the late 1970s and early 1980s, the situation had become so grim in the steelmaking portion of KSC's portfolio that the Oakland office became more determined to find a buyer for Fontana. While KSC was losing money hand over fist and shouldered great debt, in the early 1980s, the company still possessed assets worth hundreds of millions of dollars, giving it some allure. The Henry J. Kaiser Family Foundation, which held a 16.5 percent share of KSC's stock, created a feeding frenzy when it announced its plan to sell its KSC stock, first to investor Roger Tamraz in 1981. Tamraz offered $47.87 per share, but the deal fell through when Tamraz demanded a seat on the company's board of directors. A few months later, the foundation then offered KSC investor Stanley Hiller its stock for $50 per share. When this did not receive stockholder approval, he upped the offer to $52, then to $53, then eventually to $55.25 per share in 1982. This amount seemed to satisfy all the parties involved, but as the deal neared completion, Hiller backed out. It seems that a closer inspection of the company's ledgers revealed that the $403 million purchase price was not such a good deal for Hiller after all. The asset-rich, debt-heavy, earnings-challenged Kaiser Steel was attractive to the right kind of investor, especially one looking to cleave off small bits; one observer called it "an industrial flea market."

One basic problem facing the board was that the western steel market had seen growth over the last twenty years, but much of that increase had been gobbled up by foreign steelmakers. From 1970 to 1979, for example, imported steel tonnage rose from 2.4 million tons to 3.5 million tons in Kaiser's seven western states market, while KSC's steel production remained flat. And imported steel sometimes sold for one hundred dollars less per ton than that of KSC. The federal government's attempts at shielding domestic steelmakers by confronting foreign producers over the years had failed. From 1969 to 1974, the federal government (through the U.S. International Trade Commission) maintained voluntary restraints with foreign steel exporters, but overseas mills compensated for the restrictions by shifting their mix of steel to higher profit items. After the crash of 1975, though, the industry and labor revived demands for government intervention. To prevent a trade war that could come out of placing duties on imported steel, the U.S. government instituted a "trigger mechanism" in 1978. The regulatory machinery went into effect if an American producer brought charges against an overseas steel producer. The government calculated what it probably cost an efficient foreign mill to produce and deliver steel here, then it initiated ("triggered") an investigation of "dumping" and finally levied fines against the producer if found guilty. Given the ever-changing steel market of the time, oscillating currency exchange rates and changes in costs of materials and energy, the results were not overwhelming. With the trigger invoked so infrequently, Washington suspended the mechanism after a few years. The federal retreat left domestic steelmakers, especially the vulnerable integrated producers, struggling to remain competitive, at the mercy of market forces, which could change wildly and quickly. The conservative Ronald Reagan administration, not ideologically comfortable with trade restrictions on principle but facing an increasingly worried American public in an election year, negotiated the Voluntary Exports Restrictions Agreement (VERA) with major steel-exporting nations in 1984.

In November 1981, Kaiser Steel's board of directors announced that the company would end integrated steelmaking by 1983, ending years of speculation. Fontana would no longer lay claim to being the West Coast's only mine-to-metal steel plant. The very thing that Henry J. had insisted on when he founded the company—that it be integrated—had proved to be unworkable by 1980. KSC's board of directors considered three options in late 1981: (1) modernizing the entire Fontana steelworks to make it world-class, (2) closing Fontana entirely, or (3) scaling back the Fontana steelworks to become a rolling mill that purchased steel slabs from the market. The board opted for choice number three. Costs for making steel at Fontana's integrated facility were just too high in the current cutthroat world steel market, especially with Fontana's high labor, pollution control, utilities and materials costs. Furthermore, Eagle Mountain did not have many years of economical iron ore production left in it (the mine's retirement was accelerated because of millions of tons of ore going to Japanese mills in the 1960s). Total losses aside, of KSC's three divisions, two made money in 1981. The Fabricated Products Division faced a bright future with $120 million in backlogged construction and manufacturing orders up and down the Pacific Coast. Likewise, KSC's Coal Products Group turned a $12 million profit in 1981 and saw its employment rise. Then there was the Steel Manufacturing Group (the Fontana plant), which posted eighteen straight quarters of losses from 1976 through 1980, a total of $229 million in red ink. The number of people employed by Kaiser Steel skidded from 8,116 in 1979 to 5,625 in 1981. The Fontana steel plant had become a liability to the existence of the Kaiser Steel Corporation.

Wasting little time, in December 1981, just weeks after the announcement of the end of steelmaking at Fontana (and the loss of about three thousand jobs), Kaiser Steel production and maintenance workers stepped forward with their own bold "labor relations" solution to the company's woes: an employee buyout of Kaiser Steel Corporation. Local 2869 announced that it wanted to purchase the ailing steelmaker under an Employee Stock Operating Plan (ESOP). Having employees actually run the operation would probably rank as the most novel labor relations approach so far at KSC. Local USWA officials wanted to keep the entire plant open, including steelmaking facilities, saving thousands of jobs, at least on paper. But two important entities rejected it, rendering the plan stillborn. KSC's Oakland leadership rejected the proposal as "neither desirable nor workable," and the USWA International office in Pittsburgh nixed it, too. All workers could seemingly do at this point was wait out the clock until the plant closed. Bethlehem Steel, B.F. Goodrich, Uniroyal, Goodyear, Firestone, U.S. Steel and General Motors all closed manufacturing facilities in Southern California in the same era. After forty years of making steel, Kaiser's Fontana plant was throwing in the towel, its managers lacking another fresh labor relations idea to defy the odds and silence the skeptics.

Chapter 7

"DRIVIN' BIG BESS DOWN"

KAISER STEEL CORPORATION AND BEYOND

The Close

When KSC's board of directors mandated, in 1981, the end of steelmaking in Fontana, it set into motion actions that wound down activity across the plant in fits and starts over an excruciating two-year period. Said a KSC manager in the *Ingot* in January 1983, "The time is drawing near when we must decide whether Fontana can ever become viable, and the decision will be based in large part on conditions over which our degree of control is limited—employment costs, import levels, and the economy." Early in 1983, Stephen Girard told readers of the *Ingot* that unforeseen turns in the steel market and the U.S. economy were not new, but recent changes were "a terrible dive." The next step—predictably, perhaps—came shortly thereafter, when on March 4, 1983, the company announced that it would cease all production at Fontana just as soon as either a suitable buyer was found or materials stockpiled at the plant had been used up. On October 25, 1983, Kaiser Steel poured its last heat of steel, bringing the total to about seventy-five million tons since 1943 and pushing seven hundred workers into the ranks of the unemployed in one fell swoop, but hundreds stayed on to roll out the steel. In fact, the company had imported slabs to fill some of the last steel orders. On Saturday, December 31, 1983, at four in the afternoon, trucks carried away what many feared would be the last steel ever to emerge from the Fontana plant. Author and Fontana native Mike Davis, in his book *City of Quartz*, called this slow and torturous process "Drivin' Big Bess Down."

While the Oakland headquarters had thrown in the towel for making steel in Fontana, talks with other companies interested in picking up pieces of the steel plant, or just the assets of the company, stepped up. Australian natural resources company CRA Ltd. expressed interest in buying the plant and resuming steelmaking. But CRA demanded serious concessions from the United Steelworkers first. The Australians wanted to "simplify" relations with the labor force before they moved forward: workers would come back to lower wages, without any of the seniority they had earned working at KSC and without the same high-paying incentives or the Long-Range Sharing Plan, and the number of job classifications would drop from thirty-two under KSC to just eight. Workers were split over the CRA offer. As reported in the United Steelworkers' newspaper *Steel Labor*, "USWA Local 2869 members, seeing an end to the life of the mill and the loss of jobs, urge[d] that the talks resume," but representatives from the union headquarters dug in their heels and refused to consider the Aussie offer. Robert Petris, USWA District 38 director, stated bluntly, "Our union has a responsibility to maintain some basic integrity. We expressed our willingness to make realistic concessions but we don't intend to sign any document that would literally give the company the absolute right to do as it darn pleased with the workers….CRA lawyers not only want concessions, they want total surrender." That was enough for CRA to terminate negotiations, but other interested parties appeared.

BANKRUPTCY AND CORPORATE RAIDERS

The company limped along for several years after steelmaking ended, with a vastly reduced workforce and a drastically curtailed product line. Through the 1980s, a handful of suitors expressed varying amounts of interest in acquiring all or parts of Kaiser Steel. Though it was saddled with huge problems, some potential investors nonetheless viewed its asset ledger and the greatly depressed price of its stock with interest. For being so poor in working capital, Kaiser Steel remained tantalizingly asset-rich in the early 1980s, and cheap ("undervalued"), too, making it ripe for hostile takeover. Corporate raiders, entities adept at finding struggling operations, then positioning themselves to enrich their own coffers by liquidating these operations' assets, fought each other to gain that access. Between 1983 and 1987, the company struggled to stay afloat by selling parts of itself.

These were very tough times for all of America's integrated steel producers, not just Kaiser. The early 1970s saw the American steel industry (and Kaiser

Steel) post record-breaking steel production figures, with national raw steel output peaking at about 150 million tons in 1973. Then the global steel crisis hit in 1975, and the large integrated companies that had historically dominated steelmaking in America were caught flat-footed. Nationwide, domestic steelmaking plummeted to just 74.6 million tons. This decline primarily affected the integrated sector. The growing "mini-mill" sector— made up of smaller, nonintegrated plants with more focused product lines, oftentimes not located in traditional steelmaking areas, using state-of-the-art technology (usually smaller electric furnaces hooked to continuous casters) and employing non-union workforces (with no yearly contracts, very few job classifications and less pay)—could in fact be highly profitable, even in the turbulent steel market of the 1980s.

J.A. Frates of Oklahoma was a serious suitor with cash in hand to offer to buy KSC, but the talks only seemed to gin up interest among other bidders, opening a feeding frenzy of sorts. Minneapolis-based Irwin Jacobs challenged Frates for control of Kaiser Steel Corporation. Jacobs got as far as signing "an agreement in principle for the acquisition of the company" with KSC's board of directors. But he did not win over Kaiser shareholders, leading to Frates topping the Jacobs offer in late 1983. Then Monty H. Rail's Perma Resources of Denver muscled into the picture as a new half partner with Frates. In 1983, the combined forces of Rial and Frates won the approval of Kaiser Steel shareholders, who accepted their fifty-two-dollar-a-share buyout offer. But that did not end the issue of who controlled Kaiser Steel. Rial bought out Frates's interest in KSC. The Frates Group had nothing to cry about, though, as it showed a $40 million profit in that short time.

Monty Rial's tenure as Kaiser Steel CEO was brief and memorable. In early 1986, KSC defaulted on many of its loans when the energy crisis of the 1980s drove down oil and coal prices. KSC's preferred stockholders accused Rial of criminal wrongdoing for selling coal at inflated prices to Kaiser Steel—coal that Kaiser clearly did not need more of. Rial's actions incensed many former employees, stockholders and even observers outside Kaiser, so his days of running Kaiser Steel predictably ground to a close.

Looking for a new leader with deep pockets, preferred shareholders fed up with Rial allied themselves with ambitious shareholder Bruce Hendry, who forced out Rial in January 1987 and assumed the position of CEO and chairman of the board after a pitched six-month struggle. Sidelined but not silenced, Rial continued sitting on KSC's board of directors. The new CEO, Hendry, did not enjoy even a brief honeymoon in his new position, however. In fact, Hendry enraged many (not the least Rial) when, just two

Studies Under Way to Determine Future

"We do not know what Kaiser Steel will look like a year from now or five years from now. We are still studying the major options available to us," Edgar F. Kaiser, Jr., told the **Ingot** during an interview at Fontana in late July.

"When the Board of Directors is faced with decisions affecting the jobs of more than 10,000 of us at Kaiser Steel, the investments of more than 16,000 stockholders and future steel supplies for more than 2,000 of our customers, we must take our time. These decisions are too important to be made quickly. No final decisions have been made yet. We must take time to assemble as much information as we can and then use our best collective business judgments to make a final decision

about the future of Kaiser Steel," Kaiser Steel's chairman and chief executive officer said.

Mr. Kaiser emphasized that we continue to face major uncertainties and problems. Steelmaking, mining and fabricating costs are continuing to rise, although our companywide cost-cutting program has helped to control the rate at which production and overhead costs are going up. Whether the market will permit future price increases which will be large enough to cover rising costs is questionable.

The future size and control of the western steel market is another question mark. Imports took nearly 60 percent of the market in May, Mr. Kaiser said, and he estimated that if imports continue at that rate,

they will set tonnage and market-share records in 1980. Foreign steel is now making serious inroads in products, such as tin plate, which have previously been supplied almost exclusively by domestic producers. At the same time, some steel industry observers expect the total national and western steel markets in 1980 to be substantially below 1979 levels.

"As you know, we have looked at a number of options to deal with these problems and to arrive at the best course of action for Kaiser Steel," Mr. Kaiser said. "We were unsuccessful in our attempts to sell or merge significant portions of our assets with either NKK or LTV Corporation. There are no other sale or merger discussions going on and we

are not aware of any other potential buyers interested in talking with us right now.

"There now seem to be two other major approaches open to us. We said at the annual meeting of stockholders that some analysts had suggested that Kaiser Steel be liquidated and that, although we had no plan for liquidation at that time, we had, of course, analyzed the possible results of liquidation. We are continuing to study that option," Mr. Kaiser said.

He also explained that in considering liquidation, the Board would take a hard look at the long-term outlook for employees, customers and stockholders if we decide to stay in business and to continue to run

(Continued on page 6)

the ingot

Kaiser Steel Corporation/August 1980

The *Ingot's* article on Edgar Kaiser Jr. coming to KSC could not have given many KSC employees hope for the continued operation of the company.

weeks into his new job, he terminated the health insurance benefits of almost six thousand Kaiser Steel employees, retirees and their surviving spouses. Affected people received a letter from Kaiser Steel stating that "Tragically, the once mighty Kaiser Steel does not have the financial ability to continue funding your medical benefits." Claimed Kaiser Steel's new CEO, "The cupboard is bare." Hendry pointed to Monty Rial's leadership and costly legal bid to retain control of the firm for depleting cash reserves. "None of this is my fault," claimed Hendry. "I'm as much a victim as anyone." Incredibly, Hendry followed up the bombshell letter with another broadside delivered in the mail to KSC retirees just days later. In this second note, Hendry stated that miscalculations in a computer program led to hundreds of retirees being given too much money in their pension payments, and Hendry wanted them to pay it back, in a lump sum or monthly payments. Twenty-five dollars would be automatically deducted from the monthly pension check of each retiree. One such retiree, Lloyd Whitt, a former crane repairman, owed KSC $426.15. An exasperated Whitt observed, "I figured it was just another rip-off. They'll keep rippin' and keep rippin' till there's nothing to rip." Embattled workers challenged the action.

Continued heavy financial losses, insufficient income, nagging debt, frustrated creditors and retirees and a successful bloodletting by corporate raiders brought about the inevitable filing for bankruptcy by Kaiser Steel Corporation on February 11, 1987. Claiming that Kaiser Steel faced some $623 million in debt, Hendry argued, "This was not our choice. We were experiencing severe creditor pressure. We really had no alternative." Chapter 11 bankruptcy protections would keep creditors at arm's length while Hendry and the board figured out how to squeeze even more money out of what was left of KSC, and a committee of major creditors formed to represent creditors' interests. Some creditors had lent huge sums to the moribund steel firm and so presented KSC with a massive bill. Secured creditors Chase Manhattan Bank of New York and GATX of Chicago demanded $60 and $20 million from Kaiser, respectively. Said Elliot Schneider, a New York–based economist who had tracked the KSC story, "It's pathetic that no better end could come. You can almost cry about what's happened to Kaiser Steel." He spread the blame widely for Kaiser's painful demise, from short-sighted management and shareholders to greedy unions and unforeseen overseas competition. "There's so much blame to spread around. There are no heroes or villains here." It is arguable whether or not Schneider was right about there being no heroes or villains, but one thing was for sure—there were certainly losers in this story. The people who had the most to lose, as well as those who lost the most, were Kaiser Steel workers. They had their jobs liquidated, then their health insurance canceled, and now, to compound their misery, many—including those well into their retirement years—had to worry about their pensions.

While corporate boardroom intrigue and changes of leadership grabbed headiness, KSC managers continued leaning on coal mining and asset sales to earn the company money. Total revenues for KSC plummeted from over $500 million in 1981 to an average of about $150 million annually for the years 1983 through 1986, but coal output tripled to over three million tons annually. And Kaiser managers sold noncoal divisions, like Myers Drum and Kaiser Steel Tubing, which netted the firm about $250 million. Kaiser was having a blowout sale: everything had to go. After its cessation of steelmaking in December 1983, Kaiser Steel no longer needed the ingredients to make metal, so managers began to ponder what to do with the vast iron mine at Eagle Mountain. There were maybe twenty to thirty years of mining left at recent production figures—but at higher costs, as the easiest ore had been extracted, and it contained only so-so iron content. KSC's 1985 annual report revealed that managers were thinking of a converting the iron

Kaiser drops another bombshell on retirees

By P.G. TORREZ
Sun Business Writer

FONTANA — Lloyd Whitt is stomping mad.

Just two days after the former Kaiser Steel Corp. crane repairman was told his medical benefits were being eliminated, the company dropped another bombshell.

On Wednesday, Whitt, 53, received a letter from his former employer saying it had miscalculated his monthly pension benefits and overpaid him since he left the company four years ago. The financially beleaguered corporation told him to return $426.15.

"I figured it was just another rip-off," Whitt said Thursday.

"They'll keep rippin' and keep

☐ **FOR SALE:** Starving for cash, Kaiser Steel Corp. announced Thursday it is putting its wholly owned coal subsidiary on the block to finance a restructuring. Story/**B12**

rippin' till there's nothing to rip," he said,

Whitt wasn't the only one who received the letter.

Frank Anglin, president of the Kaiser Steel Cares Foundation, established in 1984 to help retirees, said Kaiser's benefits department told him that between 1,000 and 1,500 letters were mailed.

Bruce E. Hendry, Kaiser's chairman and chief executive

See **KAISER/Back page**

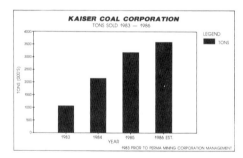

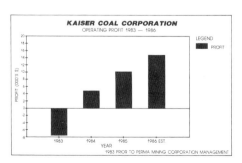

Above: Local media called the company's request for retirees to pay back money "another bombshell," which seems about right.

Left: By 1986, the company had pinned its hopes for success primarily on coal sales, as suggested by these graphs from the 1986 KSC annual report.

mine into a waste facility site for Los Angeles refuse. KSC's managers could not unload its assets fast enough to keep up with the red ink recorded by company operations and residual debt.

New Ventures from the Old Company

Kaiser Steel Corporation did not survive bankruptcy. In November 1988, Kaiser Steel Resources (KSR) emerged, a considerably smaller enterprise. Kaiser had lost its fabricating plants and coal mines during bankruptcy, leaving it with the Fontana plant, the Eagle Mountain mine and a controlling interest in the Fontana Water Company. KSR's mission statement issued in 1989 committed the firm to "maximize value to our shareholders through the development of our three valuable assets, all crucial to Southern California: land, waste management and water. We are committed to rebuilding Kaiser into a stable, solid and profitable contributor to the people and environment in California and the nation." Its management team, which consisted of some people new to Kaiser and former Kaiser execs like Gerald "Gerry" Fawcett, who had run KSC's tin mill, did not entertain serious thoughts of resurrecting integrated steel production or steel manufacturing. The leadership of the new entity dedicated itself to managing the remnants of the former steel company, suing some of the raiders that had ravaged the firm a few years before and thus scraping together whatever money it could to pay off residual debt and maybe turn a profit.

The now silent Fontana steel plant began to change in appearance rapidly as the front end of the mill was dismantled. Some of the mill, like the blast furnaces and open hearths, KSC sold for scrap. Cutting up "the Bess" to make new products like concrete reinforcing bar would have been a striking irony if it wasn't such a tragedy. Much of the finishing end, however, was left standing, functional and capable of making money. Since Kaiser Steel Resources needed to stimulate cash flow and had no interest in running a steel mill, it looked for a buyer for the finishing end of the plant. That buyer was actually a consortium calling itself California Steel Industries (CSI). California Steel agreed to pay Kaiser Steel Resources about $120 million for the BOP shop and caster, a handful of rolling mills and land around the old mill site. Three interests with some background in steel came together to form CSI: Michael Wilkerson, a Southern California broker and head of Pacific Steel; Companhia Vale do Rio Doce Brazil (CVRD), a Brazilian iron

Kaiser Steel Resources' (KSR) primary moneymakers (Eagle Mountain, the plant site and water rights) dominated the company's 1993 annual report cover.

ore exporter; and Kawasaki Corporation, Japan's third-largest steelmaker. The Brazilian firm, a state-owned enterprise that also operated a steel mill yoked with a surplus of steelmaking capacity, looked to CSI as a recipient of its unfinished slabs. Wilkerson soon sold his interest in the venture, however, leaving just the Brazilians and Japanese in charge. The former Kaiser Steel had become the first American integrated steel producer seeking purchase by a foreign company in 1979, and the remnants of the Fontana plant became the first fully foreign-owned flat-rolled steel producer in the risky U.S. and world steel market of the late twentieth century.

California Steel Industries was no clone of Kaiser Steel, but it relied on an important infusion of former KSC workers to launch its operation in 1984. Kaiser's rolling mills had been mothballed and maintained since Fontana closed, so CSI officials hoped that, after minimal reconditioning, they could soon produce steel products again. The appeal of a job at a steel plant drew thousands to apply for work at the new company in the summer of 1984, even amid rumors that the wage rate might be half of that paid by Kaiser. *Steel Labor* reported that more than three thousand people applied for about 450 jobs at CSI before it commenced production, some motivated applicants spending the night in sleeping bags and enduring hours in line under a hot sun. Production began quickly, customers lined up and CSI added more jobs. Soon the new rolling mill had about nine hundred workers on the payroll, most of them former Kaiser Steel workers. Naturally, with so many former KSC workers who had been union members, the United Steelworkers confidently approached organizing CSI employees. Yet in spite of the determined efforts of dedicated union people, the union's effort to organize the new workforce failed convincingly. In his book *City of Quartz,* Mike Davis reports that a staggering 88 percent of CSI workers rejected joining the United Steelworkers. Residual hostility toward the union from rank-and-file Kaiser workers was widespread, even if it had not been fully aired before. The controversial last president of USWA Local 2869, Frank Anglin, saw the lopsided vote and rejection coming, saying, "There was a lot of bitterness from employees when the international [the Pittsburgh USWA headquarters] refused to give up any concessions to Kaiser that we had voted in our local in 1980." These former Kaiser Steel workers felt their unions had failed them by being too proud and inflexible to make concessions, their leaders too concerned about getting reelected to make tough decisions to keep mills open.

Navigating the treacherous waters of the late twentieth-century steel market, CSI has carved out a respectable niche for itself on the West Coast, although at times its management has seemed restless. After CSI purchased KSC's rolling mills, it produced a targeted array of steel products, built its workforce up to about one thousand and, in the 1980s and '90s, rolled about one million tons of steel annually and generated about $500 million in revenue yearly, an impressive record. But rumors swirled of CSI bringing steelmaking back to Fontana. Selling the relatively new $250 million BOP Shop No. 2 in 1992 to foreign steelmakers suggested that steelmaking in Fontana was done—but maybe not. When CSI acquired Kaiser's rolling mills, it continued ongoing negotiations with the Capital Iron and Steel Corporation of the People's Republic of China. CSI's vice president Matthew McFadden put it simply: "It's a good deal for both sides. We can't run that facility here." CSI sold the modern steelmaking mill to the Chinese firm for about $15 million, less than 10 percent what it cost to build. Considering the worldwide surplus of steel capacity, CSI officials felt happy to sell the $250 million mill for the price it got. *TIME* magazine reported that the Chinese would spend some $400 million dismantling, labeling, moving and reconstructing the steelmaking shop. Chinese workers did most of the dismantling. U.S. congressman George Brown (D–San Bernardino), tried to calm upset constituents who had hoped to do some of the heavy lifting themselves: "The sale was absolutely conditional on the Chinese workers disassembling it because they will reassemble it." The three hundred Chinese workers packing up BOP Shop No. 2 spent some money on lodging and food, circulating a bit of money locally. Over the next couple of years, the Chinese crew labored on the massive facility, steadily shrinking the structure on the other side of a chain link and barbed wire fence that enclosed the area.

Still, the rumors of steelmaking returning to Fontana persisted. One early rumor came from the ranks of labor: *Steel Labor* reported that "Kawasaki is said to be in a position to provide technology strategies to help revive the production of the plant." Validating the scuttlebutt in a vague way, CSI official Howard Wilkinson said that management was indeed considering bringing back steelmaking to Fontana, but he elaborated little to the *Los Angeles Times*, saying it would take about two years and considerable financing, but "it is something we want to do." Being a privately owned firm, CSI does not have publicly report its financial performance.

Then in June 1993, CSI shocked the public when it announced an ambitious plan to add high-tech steelmaking to its operations. After a decade of profitably rolling imported slabs, CSI announced its intention to install an electric arc furnace at the Fontana rolling mill to melt Southern California scrap and make steel. Linked to a continuous caster, the new furnace would be able to provide a more reliable supply of steel to CSI's rolling mills, and it carried a $220 million price tag. CSI's announced expansion utilized current steelmaking technology, which is in part what allowed mini-mills their impressive success. An excited California governor

The east pit in the former Eagle Mountain mine, which KSR estimated could accept trash from Los Angeles for over seventy years.

Pete Wilson was on hand to give the event some sparkle, and he committed "a team of red-tape cutters" to CSI to expedite the review and regulatory process. With expansion envisioned to add perhaps 3,500 related jobs outside of CSI and steer over $1 billion to Sacramento tax coffers, the optics of the project appeared to be well worth the governor's time. "We're going to build a steel mill in California," Wilson promised, "and it's going to send a message around the country and the world that California is coming back." But when competitor Nucor backed off from its threat to build a new furnace in the Pacific Northwest the next year, CSI similarly retracted its plans; the excitement created by the expansion announcement died as quickly as it had flared up.

While CSI rolled imported steel, Kaiser Steel Resources kept busy squeezing small amounts of income from the old Fontana plant. At any one time, a few dozen companies used the plant site for things like parking truck trailers, housing hazardous waste (some recovered there) and shredding old tires. Fontana mill's gigantic piles of slag, over ten million cubic yards of the porous gravel heaped into two medium-sized mountains on the plant site, found buyers looking for concrete-making materials, railroad ballast and trace amounts of metals the by-product still contained. One novel source of cash for KSR came from renting out the old plant as a backdrop for filming movies, TV shows, commercials and music videos. Forty years of steel production had left large portions of the site pocked with tar pits and piles of asbestos and heavy metals, with areas of earth foul smelling and darkly stained. Not surprisingly, therefore, the Environmental Protection Agency red-flagged the plant site, and the expansive and expensive cleanup continued while KSR managers developed long-term plans for the real estate. Originally, management planned to build an industrial park on a large piece of their 1,100-plus-acre parcel, and in 1988, KSR entered into an agreement with a major Southern California land developer, the Lusk Company, to do just that. However, with a sharp business recession muddying the prospects of the park drawing sufficient interest, in 1992, KSR scaled back its site plans with Lusk and moved in a new direction. Shifting gears quickly, Kaiser Steel Resources began developing plans for a racetrack on the land. In 1994, Kaiser (after changing its name to Kaiser Resources and then to Kaiser Ventures, hereafter referred to as KV) announced a joint deal to build and operate a major automobile racetrack with Penske Motorsports. Workers scooped up some three thousand cubic feet of soil laden with contaminants and hauled it away. A "cap" of two feet of clean soil and a polyethylene sheet was placed over earth with residual contamination. The EPA and

Left: CSI's announcement it would bring back steelmaking to Fontana drew considerable interest from officials like Governor Pete Wilson, 1993.

Right: Kaiser Venture's (KV) development of part of the former plant site into a high-profile racetrack made the cover of KV's 1995 annual report.

California's Department of Toxic Substances Control finally granted the site a clean bill of health, construction sped forward and the $100 million California Speedway (later called the Auto Club Speedway) held its first race in 1997. The two-mile oval track attracts premier racing, including NASCAR- and CART-sponsored races, and has a seating capacity of eighty thousand spectators. As a part of the Kaiser Steel legacy slipped away in 1997, in 1998, a new one appeared: the Henry J. Kaiser High School in Fontana. The school not only used the name of the company founder but also the company's motto "Together We Build."

Moving forward, the 11,350-acre Eagle Mountain mine posed interesting revenue generation possibilities. Like the Fontana plant, Eagle Mountain occasionally served as a TV and film set, but that was not a long-term deal. The quick transformation of the mine and town into a minimum-security jail provided some income. The barren and isolated location guaranteed low costs, few complaints from worried neighbors and a natural deterrent to escape. The prison operated from 1988 until 2013. Then KSR entered into an agreement with the Mine Reclamation Corporation to transform

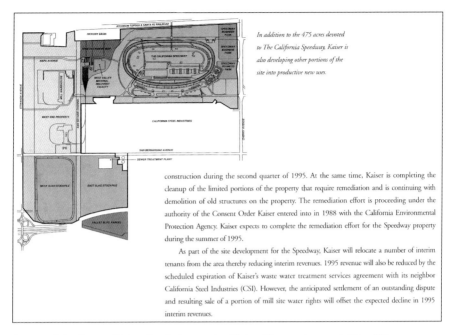

In addition to the 475 acres devoted to The California Speedway, Kaiser is also developing other portions of the site into productive new uses.

construction during the second quarter of 1995. At the same time, Kaiser is completing the cleanup of the limited portions of the property that require remediation and is continuing with demolition of old structures on the property. The remediation effort is proceeding under the authority of the Consent Order Kaiser entered into in 1988 with the California Environmental Protection Agency. Kaiser expects to complete the remediation effort for the Speedway property during the summer of 1995.

As part of the site development for the Speedway, Kaiser will relocate a number of interim tenants from the area thereby reducing interim revenues. 1995 revenue will also be reduced by the scheduled expiration of Kaiser's waste water treatment services agreement with its neighbor California Steel Industries (CSI). However, the anticipated settlement of an outstanding dispute and resulting sale of a portion of mill site water rights will offset the expected decline in 1995 interim revenues.

A map of the former Kaiser Steel plant under Kaiser Ventures' control. The 475-acre area made into a track still left hundreds of acres to develop.

the abandoned mine into a state-of-the-art landfill and materials recycling facility. With Southern California's growth continuing unabated, the idea sounded like a winner. Eagle Mountain had enough capacity to accept twenty thousand tons of trash daily for over seventy-five years. Low-cost rail transportation would carry the trash to a fully lined pit, engineered to catch liquid runoff. This Eagle Mountain possibility reanimated one of Henry J.'s favorite adages: "Find a need and fill it." Kaiser signed a one-hundred-year lease with the reclamation company, which would develop the site and provide Kaiser a monthly lease payment of over $100,000, then additional fees when the trash started arriving. But transforming a mine into a landfill is complicated and expensive, which led to Kaiser Ventures declaring bankruptcy in 2011. What emerged shed itself of the Kaiser name entirely, so Kaiser Ventures was the final derivative of Kaiser Company, Iron and Steel Division, founded in 1940. The new firm adopted the innocuous acronym CIL&D (which was still based in Ontario, as was Kaiser Ventures, a few miles from Fontana) and fronted a new plan for Eagle Mountain. They found a buyer, Eagle Crest, which paid $25 million for the site in 2016. Santa

Monica–based Eagle Crest Energy's plans would take Eagle Mountain development in the completely new direction of electricity production. This proposal would use underground water and solar energy to produce steam, which would turn turbines and make electricity, then convert the steam back into water and force it back underground in a "closed loop" system. As of this writing, the fate of Eagle Mountain mine is still unfolding.

As for Kaiser's workers, they have struggled and survived. In fact, Kaiser steelworkers have displayed an amazing cohesiveness and spirit of cooperation in the wake of the plant closure and bankruptcy. Between 1983 and 1987, the fate of Kaiser Steel employee health and life insurance benefits fell into considerable doubt as company assets evaporated and pressing debt threatened the company's viability. Worker retirement pensions received protection from the federal government through the Pension Benefits Guarantee Corporation (PBGC), and hourly workers received benefits from the United Steelworkers, but KSC retirees still faced huge losses in their other benefits; if the company pulled coverage for health insurance, the estimated value lost ran as high as $500 million. Government regulation of bankruptcy prohibits companies from reneging on worker benefits if the company is solvent, or even if they are closed and out of business (through the so-called Metzenbaum amendments), but the laws are not so clear if companies are bankrupt and still operating in some capacity. Kaiser Steel fell into this uncertain category. While being picked over by raiders in the 1980s, KSC remained open, albeit at an eviscerated capacity, and therefore unaffected by the Metzenbaum amendments protecting benefits, so Bruce Hendry possibly acted within the law when he canceled health insurance protection in 1987. Since under some bankruptcy protection chapters, health and life insurance benefits are not protected, Kaiser Steel retirees had a great deal of interest in which road the company took under reorganization. For instance, if Kaiser had filed for Chapter 7 protection in 1987, which management had indeed considered, Kaiser workers would have lost their benefits protection, so they strongly favored the company filling Chapter 11 protection, which did have that coverage. This explains the immense pleasure retirees expressed when they gained a seat on the board during bankruptcy proceedings, which meant they could have some voice in deciding the fate of the company and their insurance.

With so much at stake, some Kaiser Steel workers formed a group to protect the insurance coverage they retained and to sue to recover benefits taken from workers illegally. KSC retirees Nicolas Rickard, Lyle "Scotty" Stevenson, Tom Rabone and Ronnie Bitonti filed suit in September 1987

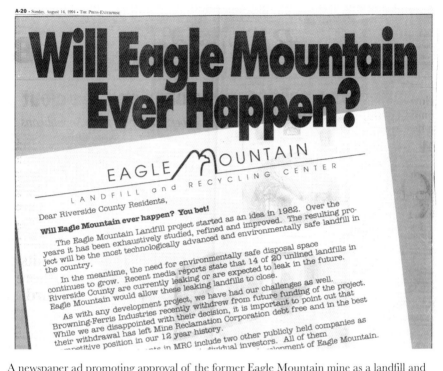

A-20 · Sunday, August 14, 1994 · THE PRESS-ENTERPRISE

Will Eagle Mountain Ever Happen?

EAGLE MOUNTAIN
LANDFILL and RECYCLING CENTER

Dear Riverside County Residents,

Will Eagle Mountain ever happen? You bet!

The Eagle Mountain Landfill project started as an idea in 1982. Over the years it has been exhaustively studied, refined and improved. The resulting project will be the most technologically advanced and environmentally safe landfill in the country.

In the meantime, the need for environmentally safe disposal space continues to grow. Recent media reports state that 14 of 20 unlined landfills in Riverside County are currently leaking or are expected to leak in the future. Eagle Mountain would allow these leaking landfills to close.

As with any development project, we have had our challenges as well. Browning-Ferris Industries recently withdrew from future funding of the project. While we are disappointed with their decision, it is important to point out that their withdrawal has left Mine Reclamation Corporation debt free and in the best competitive position in our 12 year history.

...nts in MRC include two other publicly held companies as ...dividual investors. All of them ...lopment of Eagle Mountain.

A newspaper ad promoting approval of the former Eagle Mountain mine as a landfill and energy producer.

against Kaiser Steel to prevent management from choosing Chapter 7 protection. Then these and other retirees established the Kaiser Volunteer Employee Benefits Association (Kaiser VEBA) "to administer funds received in the settlement and to be received under the provision of the Corporation's plan of reorganization, which funds are required to pay the cost of benefits provided under this plan." Kaiser VEBA lumped together the individual claims retirees filed and formed a trust, which attempted to recover as much money as possible. While Kaiser VEBA could not reverse the stripping of Kaiser Steel assets, it successfully recovered millions of dollars in damages from raiders, which VEBA fed back into retiree benefits.

Another major KSC retiree organization, called the Fontana Oldtimers Foundation, traces its origins back to the early 1960s but also underscores the cooperative spirit running through Kaiser Steel's history. The Foundation has gone through a name change or two, but its mission to serve has remained. Technically, it never was a Kaiser Steel retiree organization, but it was dominated by these very people for years. The Oldtimers Foundation has addressed the needs of the elderly in Fontana, broadly speaking, but given

the ingot

Kaiser Steel Corporation/June 1980

KSC Places Bridge Girders In Bay Area

The first vehicular crossing of San Francisco Bay is nearing retirement after 51 years of service to Bay Area commuters, and Kaiser Steel is working on its replacement. On May 14, Kaiser Steel crews set the first of 32 massive steel girders for the main channel spans of the new Dumbarton Bridge.

The 29-foot-wide girders vary in weight from 130 to 236 tons, and in length from 199 feet to 242 feet. Using a total of approximately 4,500 tons of Kaiser steel plate, the girders were fabricated at the Fontana structural fabricating shop and assembled at the Vallejo Marine Assembly Yard.

Kaiser Steel's own barges transported the girders 47.5 miles from the Vallejo assembly site to the site of the new bridge, approximately 24 miles south of San Francisco. Construction of the new Dumbarton Bridge is proceeding about 90 feet north of and parallel to the present bridge.

Kaiser Steel's derrick barge, the "Maddie B." carefully places the first of 32 Kaiser Steel-fabricated girders atop concrete pilings for the new Dumbarton Bridge. Traffic continues on the present Dumbarton Bridge, shown on the right, which crosses San Francisco Bay at its southern end.

KSC, LTV Begin Discussions

Employment Drops In Steel Industry

Kaiser Steel's legacy can be found in structures across the West, like this bridge on San Francisco Bay; note the reference to KSC-LTV talks and steel jobs decline.

Measuring about four inches long and two inches high, this figurine, which did not always come with the plaque, has been a popular keepsake since the 1940s.

KAISER FOUNDATION HOSPITAL

Matchless Medical Care

Kaiser, an accredited general hospital with 231 beds, offers general hospital and emergency care for residents in this area who belong to the Kaiser Plan. It also furnishes emergency services to those members of the community who are not participating in the plan.

Opened in 1943, the hospital has been operated by a nonprofit corporation, Kaiser Foundation Hospitals, Inc., since 1954. In 1972, a new four-story structure will be completed, which will include 125 private rooms, eight surgical suites, three delivery rooms, and other supporting facilities, bringing the total bed capacity to 303.

The staff is supplemented by 127 doctors and surgeons of the Southern California Permanente Medical Group. In addition to the Fontana outpatient facilities, clinics are also located in Riverside, San Bernardino, and Ontario.

9961 Sierra Ave., Fontana
Phone 822-3371

The Henry Kaiser and Kaiser Steel legacies are tangibly seen in the healthcare still provided by Kaiser facilities in Fontana and beyond.

the overwhelming presence of Kaiser Steel Corporation in Fontana through the 1970s into the 1980s, Kaiser retirees took most of the leadership roles, provided most of the volunteer labor and used most of the services provided. For years, in the late twentieth century, hundreds of volunteers, almost all of retirement age, performed household repairs and light construction on local residences. The Oldtimers Foundation has operated a nutrition center in Fontana, open to all seniors at a nominal cost. More ambitious than that, perhaps, it also owns and operates senior citizen residential complexes around Fontana, with a large building named after USWA Local 2869 president Dino Papavero. As the volunteers and leaders of the Oldtimers Foundation who worked at Kaiser Steel have grayed and passed, new non-Kaiser-related people have supplanted them, but for the immediate future, Kaiser's stamp on this group and area remains indelible.

BIBLIOGRAPHY

Audiotape Interviews

All interviews are at the Fontana Historical Society.

Alvin, Cass. June 24, 1994.
Anthony, Mark. February 6, 1994.
Bitonti, Ronald. January 27, 1994; July 22, 1994.
Covert, Timon "Curly." April 22, 1994; June 23, 1994.
Foust, Mildred. June 8, 1993.
Heaton, Gussie. July 29, 1994
Luksich, Minnie. June 8, 1993; August 22, 1994
Maxie, Vern. May 10, 1993
Piazza, John. May 27, 1993.
Rabone, Tom. January 17, 1994; July 29, 1994.
Rothstein, Abe. August 9, 1994.
Trunoske, John. August 9, 1994.
Wells, Dorothy. July 22, 1994.

Books

Brody, David. *In Labor's Cause: Main Themes on the History of the American Worker.*
   New York: Oxford University Press, 1993.

Cadwell, Ernest, ed. *History of Fontana*. San Bernardino County Historical Society and the Fontana Chamber of Commerce, 1955.

Davis, Mike. *City of Quartz: Excavating the Future in Los Angeles*. New York: Verso, 1990.

Foster, Mark S. *Henry J. Kaiser: Builder in the Modern American West*. Austin: University of Texas Press, 1989.

Gregory, Chester W. *Women in Defense Work during World War II*. New York: Exposition Press, 1974.

Grether, E.T. *The Steel and Steel-Using Industries of California: Prewar Developments, Wartime Adjustments, and Long-Term Outlook*. Sacramento: California State Printing Office, 1946.

Heiner, Albert P. *Henry J. Kaiser: Western Colossus, An Insider's View*. San Francisco, CA: Halo Press, 1991.

Hogan, William T. *Economic History of the Iron and Steel Industry in the United States*. 5 vols. Lexington, MA: D.C. Heath & Co., 1971.

Kesselman, Amy. *Fleeting Opportunities: Women Shipyard Workers in Portland and Vancouver during World War II and Reconversion*. Albany: State University of New York Press, 1990.

Labor in California: Biennial Statistical Report to the Legislature, 1939–1940. Sacramento: California State Printing Office, 1941.

Langworth, Richard M. *Kaiser-Frazer: The Last Onslaught on Detroit*. Kutztown, PA: Automobile Quarterly Publications, 1975.

McDonald, David J. *Union Man*. New York: E.P. Dutton and Co., 1969.

Milkman, Ruth. *Gender at Work: The Dynamics of Job Discrimination by Sex during World War II*. Urbana: University of Illinois Press, 1987.

Nash, Gerald D. *The American West Transformed: The Impact of the Second World War*. Bloomington: Indiana University Press, 1985.

Sweeney, Vincent. *The United Steelworkers of America: Twenty Years Later 1936–1956*. n.p.: 1956.

Warren, Kenneth. *The American Steel Industry, 1850–1970: A Geographical Interpretation*. Oxford: Clarendon Press, 1973.

Company Publications

All company publications—such as pamphlets, internal memos, speeches by executives, etc.—are at the Fontana Historical Society.

Journal and Magazine Articles

Articles used are at the Fontana Historical Society.

"The Arrival of Henry Kaiser." *Fortune*, July 1951, 68–73, 141–54.

"As the 'Lone Wolf' Tells It…" *Newsweek*, November 9, 1959, 104–6.

"Complexity May Undo Kaiser Sharing Plan." *Industry Week*, February 14, 1972, 14.

"The Earth Movers II: They Turn to Shipbuilding and Change the Face of the West." *Fortune*, September 1943, 118–23; 219–26.

Grattan, C. Hartley. "The Future of the Pacific Coast: I. California's Prospects." *Harper's*, March 1945, 301–10.

"Industry Wary of Kaiser Plan." *Iron Age*, December 27, 1962, 30–31.

Jacoby, Sanford, and Daniel Mitchell. "Management Attitudes toward Two-Tier Pay Plans." *Journal of Labor Research* 7 (Summer 1986): 221–38.

"Mapping a Steel Peace." *Business Week*, March 19, 1960, 29–30.

Post, Charles T. "Is It the Last Gasp for Henry J. Kaiser's Fontana 'Love Child?'" *Iron Age*, January 22, 1982, 24–29.

"Steel Has Its Eyes on Washington." *Business Week*, July 22, 1961, 102–3.

"Steel in the West." *Fortune*, February 1945, 130–33.

Newspapers

Articles used are at the Fontana Historical Society.

Fontana (CA) Herald-News
Ingot
Labor Herald
Los Angeles (CA) Times
Ontario (CA) Daily Report
San Bernardino (CA) Sun
Snorter
Riverside (CA) Daily Press
Riverside (CA) Press Enterprise
Steel Labor
Wall Street Journal

ABOUT THE AUTHOR

Ric Dias was born and raised in Northern California, nowhere near Fontana, so he was introduced to the Kaiser family of businesses by seeing Kaiser automobiles and pink and fuchsia Kaiser Sand & Gravel trucks on the road in the 1960s and '70s. In the '80s and '90s, he attended graduate school at the University of California, Riverside, which is about twenty miles from the former Fontana steel plant, and there became familiar with the Kaiser Steel story. He received a PhD in history from UC Riverside in 1995 and since then has been a professor of history at Northern State University in Aberdeen, South Dakota. He has written several articles on Kaiser Steel, as well as a book and articles on California engine maker Hall-Scott, and he has owned a 1951 Kaiser automobile since 1981.